CW00957709

The Taming of the Shrew

by William Shakespeare

Martin Old

Series Editors:
Nicola Onyett and Luke McBratney

HODDER
EDUCATION
AN HACHETTE UK COMPANY

The publisher would like to thank the following for permission to reproduce copyright material:

Acknowledgements:

pp.4, 5: From *The Bible*; **p.6: Robert Burton:** from *The Anatomy of Melancholy* (1624); **p.7:** From 'The Frolicsome Duke' (19th Century); **p.7: Annabel Patterson:** from 'Framing the Taming' from *Shakespeare and Cultural Traditions*, eds. Tetsuo Kishi, Roger Pringle, Stanley Wells (University of Delaware Press, 1994); **pp.22, 23: Phillip Stubbes:** from *Anatomy of the Abuses in England, Vol. 1: Shakspere's Youth* (1583); **p.34: Emperor Justinian:** from the 'Code of Justinian' (529–34); **p.38: William Shakespeare:** from *The Taming of the Shrew (Arden Shakespeare)*, ed. Brian Morris (Methuen, 1981); p.38: Caroline Spurgeon: from *Shakespeare's Imagery and What it Tells Us* (Martino Fine Books, 1935); **p.39: Gerald Lascelles:** from *Shakespeare's England* (OUP, 1966); **pp.45, 46: Rebecca Warren and William Shakespeare:** from *The Taming of the Shrew: York Notes Advanced* (Longman, 2005); **p.59: Jan Harold Brunvand:** adapted summary of dissertation entitled 'The Taming of the Shrew: A Comparative Study of Oral and Literary Versions' (Aarne-Thompson Type 901, 1961); **p.63: James Edward Grant:** from *McLintock!* (Batjac Productions, 13th November 1963); **p.66: Charles Marowitz:** as cited in *Taming of the Shrew* by Graham Holderness (Manchester University Press, 1991); **p.69: John Knox:** from *First Blast of the Trumpet against the Monstrous Regiment of Women* (1558); **p.69: Roy Strong:** from *The Spirit of Britain: A Narrative History of the Arts* (Jonathan Cape, 1999); **p.72: Richard Whitford:** from *A Work for Householders* (1530); **p.96: Erin Furstnau:** from 'Feminist Themes in and Critiques of Shakespeare's Taming of the Shrew' (Cedar Crest College), www2.cedarcrest.edu/academic/eng/lfletcher/shrew/efurstnau.htm.

Every effort has been made to trace or contact all copyright holders, but if any have been inadvertently overlooked the Publishers will be pleased to make the necessary arrangements at the first opportunity.

Photo credits:

p.31 © Alastair Muir/REX Shutterstock; **p.34** © INTERFOTO/Alamy; **p.35 and p.36** © World History Archive/TopFoto; **p.39** Royal Collection Trust/© Her Majesty Queen Elizabeth II 2015; **p.40** © The Granger Collection/TopFoto; **p.42** © The Granger Collection/TopFoto; **p.64** © AF archive/Alamy; **p.65** © Nigel Norrington/ArenaPAL/TopFoto; **p.68** © World History Archive/TopFoto

Although every effort has been made to ensure that website addresses are correct at time of going to press, Hodder Education cannot be held responsible for the content of any website mentioned. It is sometimes possible to find a relocated web page by typing in the address of the home page for a website in the URL window of your browser.

Orders: please contact Bookpoint Ltd, 130 Milton Park, Abingdon, Oxon OX14 4SB. Telephone: (44) 01235 827720. Fax: (44) 01235 400454. Lines are open 9.00–17.00, Monday to Saturday, with a 24-hour message answering service. Visit our website at www.hoddereducation.co.uk

© Martin Old 2016

First published in 2016 by

Hodder Education

An Hachette UK Company,

Carmelite House, 50 Victoria Embankment

London EC4Y 0DZ

Impression number	5	4	3	2	1
Year	2020	2019	2018	2017	2016

All rights reserved. Apart from any use permitted under UK copyright law, no part of this publication may be reproduced or transmitted in any form or by any means, electronic or mechanical, including photocopying and recording, or held within any information storage and retrieval system, without permission in writing from the publisher or under licence from the Copyright Licensing Agency Limited. Further details of such licences (for reprographic reproduction) may be obtained from the Copyright Licensing Agency Limited, Saffron House, 6–10 Kirby Street, London EC1N 8TS.

Cover photo (and throughout) © Getty Images/WIN-Initiative RM

Typeset in 11/13pt Univers LT Std 47 Light Condensed by Integra Software Services Pvt. Ltd., Pondicherry, India

Printed in Italy

A catalogue record for this title is available from the British Library

ISBN 9781471854132

Contents

Using this guide iv

Introduction vi

1   Synopsis 1

2   Scene summaries and commentaries 4

3   Themes 29

4   Characters 43

5   Writer's methods: Form, structure and language 51

6   Contexts 57

7   Working with the text 77

    Assessment Objectives and skills 77

    Building skills 1: Structuring your writing 77

    Building skills 2: Analysing texts in detail 86

    Extended commentaries 88

    Top ten quotations 91

    Taking it further 99

Why read this guide?

The purposes of this A-level Literature Guide are to enable you to organise your thoughts and responses to the text, deepen your understanding of key features and aspects and help you to address the particular requirements of examination questions and non-exam assessment tasks in order to obtain the best possible grade. It will also prove useful to those of you writing an NEA piece on the text as it provides a number of summaries, lists, analyses and references to help with the content and construction of the assignment.

Note that teachers and examiners are seeking above all else evidence of an *informed personal response to the text.* A guide such as this can help you to understand the text, form your own opinions, and suggest areas to think about, but it cannot replace your own ideas and responses as an informed and autonomous reader.

Line and scene references in this guide refer to the Arden Shakespeare edition of *The Taming of the Shrew* edited by Barbara Hodgdon (2010). This edition has excellent introductory material and some notes. Where a publication is given in the **Taking it further** section on pages 99–104, the author's surname and publication date only are cited after the first full reference.

How to make the most of this guide

You may find it useful to read sections of this guide when you need them, rather than reading it from start to finish. For example, you may find it helpful to read the **Contexts** section before you start reading the text, or to read the **Scene summaries and commentaries** section in conjunction with the text – whether to back up your first reading of it at school or college or to help you revise. The sections relating to the Assessment Objectives will be especially useful in the weeks leading up to the exam.

This guide is designed to help you to raise your achievement in your examination response to *The Taming of the Shrew*. It is intended for you to use throughout your AS/A-level English literature course. It will help you when you are studying the play for the first time and also during your revision.

The following features have been used throughout this guide to help you focus your understanding of the play:

Context

Context boxes give contextual information that relates directly to particular aspects of the text.

TASK

Tasks are short and focused. They allow you to engage directly with a particular aspect of the text.

CRITICAL VIEW

Critical view boxes highlight a particular critical viewpoint that is relevant to an aspect of the main text. This allows you to develop the higher-level skills needed to come up with your own interpretation of a text.

Build critical skills

Broaden your thinking about the text by answering the questions in the **Build critical skills** boxes. These help you to consider your own opinions in order to develop your skills of criticism and analysis.

Taking it further ▶▶

Taking it further boxes suggest and provide further background or illuminating parallels to the text.

Top ten quotation

Top ten quotation

A cross-reference to Top ten quotations (see pages 91–98 of this guide), where each quotation is accompanied by a commentary that shows why it is important.

The Taming of the Shrew is a comedy written some time between 1590 and 1592, though it may have been given a final polish by Shakespeare as late as 1607. It appears in the First Folio of 1623 – the first 'complete works of Shakespeare' – but the history of the play has been complicated by the printing of the anonymous 1594 play *The Taming of a Shrew*. There are many similarities between *A Shrew* and *The Shrew* (see **Contexts** section, p. 57), something which has led to a colourful kaleidoscope of opinions about the play and its history. There are many different interpretations about the play, its origins, meanings, characters, values and dramatic potential, making it extremely rewarding to study.

There are many different interpretations about the play's origins, meanings, characters, values

The origins of the term 'comedy' are found in the theatres of Ancient Greece. In its early days the genre depicted conflict (*agon*) which placed two groups against each other in an amusing struggle, frequently depicting a society of young adults struggling against their elders. As the idea developed, writers began to create a comic hero of a young man confronting the values of a society populated by older law-making patriarchs who threaten his progress and aspirations. In this struggle, the young man needs to engage in ploys, ruses, stratagems or disguises which create laughter. It is an important feature of comedy that young people must win and that a sign of a new, emergent society is symbolised by marriage or the promise of marriage at the play's conclusion. *The Taming of the Shrew* is in many ways a non-conformist play: though the sub-plot featuring Bianca and Lucentio is traditional in the classic Greek sense, the main plot featuring Katherine and Petruchio is not. Petruchio (the anglicised spelling of Petruccio) does not seek to trick Katherine's father Baptista as Lucentio does but seeks Katherine's hand in marriage in an entirely socially acceptable manner. Lucentio spends most of the play in disguise, lying and conniving to win Bianca; he deceives everyone, especially Baptista and his own father Vincentio.

It is an important feature of comedy that young people must win

Petruchio states his wish to 'tame' the 'wild' Katherine and make her 'conformable'. Audiences may wonder if in any way the Petruchio–Katherine plot features the theme of disguise at all. It is interesting to consider the notion that Katherine's first manifestation of herself – unorthodox, temperamental, violent and occasionally wrong-headed – may be a disguise she has assumed 'for policy', as Petruchio says after his first meeting with her.

Human frailties and weaknesses are exaggerated in comedy. In Katherine's violence we may recognise the dangers of uncontrolled emotion; in Bianca's play-acting we may recognise the dangers of selfishness and dishonesty; in Gremio's ridiculous desire for Bianca we may recognise the dangers of marrying where there is no match in taste, age and experience. In Lucentio's behaviour we may recognise the dangers of falling in love with an idealised, invented version of a woman. In Baptista we may recognise the dangers of a dominant and over-controlling father. Perhaps in Petruchio's behaviour we may recognise the dangers of exerting so much control over another human being that she is unrecognisable from her former self. In these contexts comedy serves a didactic purpose and – beyond the laughter – is a very serious business for it is concerned with the improvement and development of civilised society and its purpose is to make us think.

Beyond the laughter, the purpose of comedy is to make us think

Shakespeare shows his audience a lot of violence in the play but, apart from one moment when Petruchio *may* physically restrain Katherine in Act 2, Scene 1, there is no male violence perpetrated against women, though directors over the years have invented it and shown it on stage as though it were part of Shakespeare's dramatic plan. Perhaps this has always been part of the problem with – and part of the joy of – *The Taming of the Shrew*. it is used as a blank page on which to write the values of the times, the actors and the directors. Albert Einstein joked to philosopher Maurice Solovine and mathematician Conrad Habicht: 'If the facts don't confirm your theory, change your facts.' Einstein knew our theories determine what we will find as evidence. This methodology of analysis has particularly dogged the reception and interpretation of *The Taming of the Shrew* and on stage the play has had dozens of metamorphoses. In the various quests to adapt it, the play itself as a coherent work of art has often been overlooked. Like Katherine's gown in Act 4, Scene 3, the text has been excessively edited and rearranged:

Petruchio: What, up and down carved like an apple tart?
              Here's snip, and nip, and cut, and slish and slash,
              Like to a cithern in a barber's shop.

This guide seeks to help students make sense of the entire play, *Shakespeare's play*. Despite the ups and downs of its stage-life and its mixed critical reception, *The Taming of the Shrew* is a brilliant example of dramatic theatre.

Christopher Sly, a drunken tinker who has broken some glasses but refuses to pay for them, is ejected from an inn by the hostess who goes off to fetch a constable. Sly falls asleep.

Some rich hunters find Sly drunk and the lord decides to trick him: by carrying him off, dressing him in finery and persuading him that he is a lord who has been 'lunatic' for seven years. Upon waking, Sly refuses to accept the subterfuge but gradually begins to think that he may be a lord. Bartholomew the page enters dressed as a woman and Sly commands 'her' to undress but the tinker is denied his erotic pleasure by the arrival of some actors. The play which they perform is *The Taming of the Shrew*.

Lucentio and his servants, Tranio and Biondello, arrive in Padua so that Lucentio can enrol at the university. Lucentio sees Bianca, Baptista Minola's younger daughter, and falls in love. Bianca already has two suitors, Gremio and Hortensio, but Baptista decrees Bianca will not be courted until her older and apparently wild sister, Katherine, is married first. Lucentio exchanges identities with Tranio so that he can gain access to Bianca while Tranio, as Lucentio, will pretend to woo Bianca.

Biondello is told that the reason behind the disguises is that Lucentio has killed a man in a quarrel just after their arrival. The characters exit; Sly is asked his opinion of the play and, after saying he wishes it were 'done', is heard and seen no more.

Petruchio and his servant Grumio arrive from Verona to visit Hortensio. After some farcical horseplay Petruchio announces that following his father's death he wants to find a rich wife. Hortensio suggests Katherine; Petruchio claims he doesn't care that she is 'shrewish' as long as marriage will make him richer. Hortensio asks for Petruchio's help in presenting him to Baptista in disguise as music tutor Licio so he can secretly court Bianca. Gremio enters with Lucentio disguised as Cambio whom he intends to offer to Baptista as a Latin tutor. Hortensio reveals that Petruchio is set to woo Katherine. With the arrival of Tranio disguised as Lucentio and Biondello, the party goes off to celebrate after agreeing that Petruchio should be rewarded for his role in clearing the way to Bianca.

In the next scene Katherine drags a bound Bianca around the stage furiously demanding which of her suitors she prefers. Baptista stops the violence and Petruchio, the suitors and 'the tutors' enter. Baptista permits Petruchio to woo Katherine and agrees that the two 'tutors' can teach his daughters. After agreeing the **dowry**, Petruchio asserts he will encounter no difficulties with Katherine but Hortensio enters with his lute smashed over his head, another victim of Katherine's violence. Petruchio woos Katherine with a combination

Context

In some editions the constable is a *headborough* but in Shakespeare's Warwickshire the term was thirdborough, which some editors retain to provide authentic local colour.

dowry: an amount of property or money provided by a bride's family and given to her husband on their marriage.

1

of reverse psychology, bluff, humour and sexual innuendo. Katherine 'strikes' Petruchio, who does not retaliate violently but continues with his plan to disorientate her, telling her he will tame her and marry her whether she consents now or not. Petruchio tells Baptista that Katherine has agreed to be married next Sunday; Katherine protests but after hearing Petruchio say that she is 'curst' for 'policy' and that he chooses 'her for himself' she offers no further argument. Petruchio exits, saying he will travel to Venice for wedding things. Tranio/ Lucentio persuades Baptista that he is wealthier than Gremio; Baptista agrees to a wedding between 'Lucentio' and Bianca as long as Lucentio's father Vincentio will confirm his son's finances.

Lucentio reveals his true identity to Bianca and declares his love. Petruchio is late for his wedding, leaving Katherine to fear she will be jilted; when he finally appears Petruchio's clothes and behaviour are outlandish. After a riotous service disrupted throughout by Petruchio, Katherine, who wishes to stay for the feast, is whisked away to her new husband's estate.

At Petruchio's house Katherine is denied food and sleep in the manner of a falconer bringing a wild hawk to hand, with Petruchio pretending all is done in 'care' of his bride. After arranging for a tailor and haberdasher to make Katherine new clothes, Petruchio finds fault and, again, she is deprived of something she values. Eventually Katherine agrees not to contradict Petruchio's views of the world, saying that whatever his version of events: 'so shall it be for Katherine'.

Bianca clearly favours Lucentio. Hortensio now determines to marry a rich widow, departing for Petruchio's 'taming school'. Via a lie that Mantuans will be executed in Padua, Tranio recruits an elderly gentleman – a pedant – to play the part of Lucentio's father Vincentio. The pedant persuades Baptista that Lucentio's claims are genuine, so the marriage between Lucentio and Bianca is agreed. Knowing that the lies will soon unravel, Tranio and Biondello arrange for a priest to marry Lucentio and Bianca who elope and marry in secret.

Petruchio, Katherine and Hortensio return to Baptista's; after an exchange between the newly-weds about whether the sun is the moon, they encounter an old man also travelling to Padua. Petruchio asks Katherine to greet the 'lovely maid'. Katherine complies and when Petruchio says it is an old man she apologises, claiming that the dazzling sunshine has affected her vision. This old man is the real Vincentio. When the travellers arrive in Padua, Vincentio is disturbed to find Tranio masquerading as Lucentio and fears foul play. Bianca and Lucentio enter and reveal their secret marriage. Though Vincentio is relieved that his son is alive, both Vincentio and Baptista are unhappy at the 'knavery' undertaken by Lucentio and Bianca but agree that the marriage is valid.

Lucentio holds a celebratory banquet. The three new husbands bet on which of their wives will obey first when sent for: Lucentio 'bids' Bianca to come and Hortensio 'entreats' his wife but both wives refuse to come. Petruchio 'commands' Katherine to come and she complies immediately.

Context

In an Elizabethan marriage service the clergyman asked the man, 'Wilt thou love her, comfort her, honour, and keep her in sickness and in health? And forsaking all others keep thee only to her, so long as you both shall live?' Though the second part was the same for the woman the first question was, 'Wilt thou obey him, serve him, love (and) honour (him)?'

Baptista, happy with Katherine's transformation, gives Petruchio a further twenty thousand crowns. After bringing the two reluctant wives on stage, Katherine gives a speech about what duties wives owe their husbands. Lucentio agrees that Petruchio has won the bet and Hortensio acknowledges his friend has 'tamed a curst shrew'. After a public kiss, Katherine and Petruchio leave the celebrations to go to bed.

Disguises: Who's who?

Beyond the 'joke' of transforming Sly into a lord, there are a number of physical disguises in the play.

Scene disguise begins	Character	Disguised as	Scene disguise ends
Induction, Scene 2	Bartholomew the page	The 'lord's' (Sly's) wife	The audience never sees Bartholomew revert to his own identity.
Act 1, Scene 1	Lucentio	Cambio, the Latin tutor	Act 5, Scene 1
Act 1, Scene 1	Tranio	Lucentio	Act 5, Scene 1
Act 2, Scene 1	Hortensio	Licio, the music tutor	Act 4, Scene 2
Act 4, Scene 2	The pedant from Mantua	Vincentio, Lucentio's father	Act 5, Scene 1

Scene summaries and commentaries

Target your thinking

- How does Shakespeare develop his themes and characters as the drama progresses? (**AO1**)
- What dramatic impact does each of the scenes have on an audience? You should keep a scene by scene diary to note the dramatic features which Shakespeare uses. (**AO2**)

Induction, Scene 1

Christopher Sly, drunkard and glass-breaker, is ejected from an alehouse and falls asleep. A lord's hunting party enters; the aristocrat decides to trick Sly by making him think that he is a lord: Sly is to be borne away, placed in the best chamber, dressed in lordly clothes, and when he wakes to be persuaded that he is a mighty aristocrat who has been lunatic. The help of a recently arrived group of travelling actors is enlisted. The actors are told that Sly is an eccentric nobleman who will benefit from watching a play.

The lord instructs his page Bartholomew to disguise himself as Sly's wife, who must pretend to be overjoyed at her husband's unexpected recovery after seven years of thinking he was a 'loathsome beggar'.

Commentary: 'The drunkard and the glutton will come to poverty, and slumber will clothe them with rags.' Proverbs 23:21.

The use of an Induction was a common device in plays written around the 1590s, though *Shrew* is the only Shakespeare play to have one. Sly's language is interesting. He is drunk and uses vernacular English with 'feeze' meaning to 'drive off' or 'hit'; however, he follows this up with a quotation from Kyd's *The Spanish Tragedy* – 'pocas palabras' – Spanish for 'few words'.

Context

The Spanish Tragedy or Hieronimo is Mad Again was written by Thomas Kyd some time between 1582 and 1592. The play established a new genre — the revenge tragedy — in English theatre. Wildly popular in its time, the plot is violent and sensational. Shakespeare borrows the idea of an Induction from Kyd.

Typically for a drunk, Sly misquotes the phrase into '*paucas pallabris*'. We may wonder how a Warwickshire drunk is familiar with Kyd and the theatre at all. In *The Taming of the Shrew* many things are not quite as they seem. The induction in *Shrew* is a type of preparation for the play proper: hunting and fortune-hunting will feature, as will notions of disguise, role-reversal and entitlement.

Context

```
William I (born Falaise, France 1028; died Rouen, 1087) was
called 'Conqueror' following his successful 1066 invasion
of England. Richard I (born Oxford 1157; died Chalus, 1199)
was King of England from 1189. His nickname Coeur de Lion
('Lionheart') was earned because of his fighting prowess.
How funny that Sly's Englishness is defined by two kings
who could speak little or no English and who spent most of
their lives abroad.
```

Sly conflates William the Conqueror with Richard the Lionheart to give us 'Richard Conqueror', a fictive king we have never had. Sly's threat to 'feeze' the hostess suggests male violence against women but in the play proper we never see an example of a man physically beating a woman. Katherine will go on to assault Bianca, Hortensio, Petruchio and Grumio before she learns to be happy or is bullied into submission, depending upon your interpretation.

In Genesis 1:26 we read, 'Then God said, "Let us make man in our image, after our likeness. And let them have dominion over the fish of the sea and over the birds of the heavens and over the livestock."'

Tudor theologians believed that this Bible verse meant that humans could use animals to supply us with food; therefore, in a sense hunting was not merely a sport but an activity given a quasi-sacred status due to biblical heritage. There is nothing sacred or even particularly noble about the lord here. However, perhaps he has a point; Sly *is* drunk and perhaps does deserve a moral lesson. Parts of the Bible warn against drunkenness: 'Wine is a mocker, strong drink a brawler, and whoever is led astray by it is not wise' (Proverbs 20:1) but other verses even in the same book appear contradictory: 'Give strong drink to the one who is perishing, and wine to those in bitter distress' (Proverbs 31:6). Therefore, another view is that the lord grossly exceeds any authority he may have over Sly and goes too far with him. The Bible does not give dominion to one class of people over others but this lord assumes it. The lord does not recognise Sly's essential humanity and it could be argued that, similarly, later in the play Katherine is 'invisible' until Petruchio sees her potential. Sly is identified as a '**swine**' and Katherine as a 'shrew' in their own environments. That both may have hidden depths to their humanity should not be lost on an audience.

The plan to dress Sly in fine robes is clearly a theatrical signpost for the many physical disguises that will follow but the trick operates on a deeper level: it is essentially a psychological experiment to alter Sly's mental state. Fine clothes will not make Sly a lord but they may make him *think* he is a lord; later in the play, when Katherine wants fine clothes and a fashionable cap, Petruchio frustrates her

Context

```
In Genesis
1:26—28,
God permits
humankind
to exercise
dominion over
the earth. The
Hebrew word
'radah' carries
the idea of
ruling, and
subduing, and
this command
was taken by
ruling elites
as evidence
that they had
dominion over
other humans as
well as animals.
```

> Top ten quotation

by initially denying them, making the point that internal change is the only change that matters: when she is 'gentle' and kind she can wear clothes that match her personality but not before because 'tis the mind that makes the body rich': clothes are mere 'baubles'. Petruchio will physically demonstrate these ideas by arriving for his wedding in a ragbag of ill-assorted clothing (see the Commentary on Act 3, Scene 2, p.17). Further levels of complexity are added with the arrival of the actors. The audience is now watching actors acting the parts of actors preparing to perform in a play for the benefit of a tinker who is in the process of being persuaded he is a lord by a lord who thought the tinker had behaved like a beast!

Despite its serious undercurrents we should not lose sight of the comedy: the lord planning to play the trick on Sly creates laughter; Bartholomew having to dress up as a woman is funny. When performed well, the scene is hilarious.

Induction, Scene 2

Sly wakes up in a beautiful bedroom in a strange house with attendants ready to provide for his every need. He requests 'small ale' and to dispel his confusion the servants reassure him that everyone is overjoyed to learn that their master has recovered following an illness which has lasted 15 years, the length of the illness having increased from seven years since the joke was originally planned.

The servants regale him with stories of his dreams containing references to his poverty and his friends with Warwickshire names. The servants mention his pictures of beautiful women and goddesses from classical mythology to arouse his sexual interest and, on cue, his supposed wife played by Bartholomew enters. Sly perhaps begins to think that he might be a lord, commanding his wife to undress and come to bed. but Bartholomew escapes by claiming that the physician has forbidden sex in case of a relapse. A servant enters to inform the group that actors are ready to entertain the household with a play. Sly, his pretend wife and others settle down to watch the play.

Commentary: Burton's *Anatomy of Melancholy* (1624) says:

> *It is reported of* Philippus Bonus *of Burgundy … (that) he would … walk disguised all about the town. It so fortuned … he found a country fellow dead drunk, snorting on a bulk; he caused his followers to bring him to his palace, and there stripping him of his old clothes, and attiring him after the court fashion, when he waked, he and they were all ready to attend upon his excellency, persuading him he was some great duke. The poor fellow admiring how he came there, was served in state all the day long; after supper he saw them dance, heard music, and the rest of those court-like pleasures: but late at night, when he was well tippled, and again fast asleep, they put on his old robes, and so conveyed him to the place where they first found him … In conclusion, after some little admiration, the poor man told his friends he had seen a vision, constantly believed it, would not otherwise be persuaded, and so the jest ended.*

The English folk song 'The Duke and the Tinker' or 'The Frolicsome Duke' seems to have grown out of this story and it seems probable that Shakespeare was

Context

Small ale contained little alcohol and was a famous thirst-quencher. Cheaper than stronger versions of ale traditionally consumed at festivities, it was safer to drink than water because brewing effectively pasteurises the drink. However, small beer can also be made from the 'mash' of stronger beer and can have as much alcoholic kick as a traditional 'mild'.

familiar with it. The song has a restorative ending not seen in the Philip the Good legend with the tinker rewarded for his pains:

> *For his glory to him so pleasant did seem,*
> *That he thought it to be but a mere golden dream;*
> *Till at length he was brought to the duke, where he sought*
> *For a pardon, as fearing he had set him at nought;*
> *But his highness he said, 'Thou'rt a jolly bold blade,*
> *Such a frolic before I think never was played.'*
>
> *Then his highness bespoke him a new suit and cloak,*
> *Which he gave for the sake of this frolicsome joke;*
> *Nay, and five-hundred pound, with ten acres of ground,*
> *'Thou shalt never,' said he, 'range the countries round,*
> *Crying "Old brass to mend!" for I'll be thy good friend,*
> *Nay, and **Joan** thy sweet wife shall my duchess attend.'*

The Kate Rusby version (you can view this on YouTube) is shorter and, like Shakespeare's play, does not have the charitable ending of the original song concluding with Sly being unceremoniously dumped back where he was found.

We do not know if the story of the Duke and the Tinker really happened or not – which seems perfect for *Shrew*.

The lord's teasing of Sly with wanton pictures certainly adds to the comedy of the scene putting Sly in the mood for sex. We get a flavour of wifely duty here too – analysed in more detail in the play proper – in Bartholomew's claim that Sly is 'My husband and my lord, my lord and husband, / I am your wife in all obedience'. However, this scene could be interpreted as promoting ungodly licentiousness as well as being a cruel trick to promise something not really on offer. We also have to take Bartholomew's feelings into account: some productions have him as a drag queen camping up the seduction; others a shy boy being coerced into something against his will.

Sly's sense of self is disrupted by the trick and though he still wants 'small ale' and wants his 'wife' to 'come to bed', his perceptions are altering along with the ways he describes the world. He may be beginning to believe that he is in fact a lord.

CRITICAL VIEW

In *The Taming of a Shrew* (1594 Quarto) Sly thinks he will watch a 'commodity' rather than a 'comonty' – Sly's mispronunciation of the word comedy. In *Framing the Taming* (1994), feminist Annabel Patterson argues therefore that the play is about 'advantage, profit, self-interest … Sly has somehow perceived … that the play he is about to see is not only about the commodification of women but is itself a commodity.' Patterson therefore assumes *A Shrew* is merely an alternative form of *The Shrew*: a contentious and perhaps entirely invalid assumption.

Joan: Sly asks Bartholomew if he is to call 'her' Alice Madam or Joan Madam, both common female names in Tudor England and frequently associated with women from the lowest rungs on the social hierarchy.

Context

Philip the Good (1396–1467) was Duke of Burgundy as Philip III from 1419. During his reign Burgundy reached the height of its power, becoming a hub of the civilised arts. Philip was a great administrative reformer and patron of such Flemish painters as Jan van Eyck. Famously he captured Joan of Arc in 1430 and gave her to his English allies.

Before they settle, Sly asks if it is 'household stuff' they are about to watch. The usual usage of the term described furniture, so part of the theatrical in-joke here is that the actors are about as believable in their roles as pieces of furniture. Joking apart, Shakespeare also gives the audience an early signpost for Petruchio's reference to Katherine as his 'household-stuff' in Act 3, Scene 2, line 232.

Perhaps in Induction 1 the audience did not identify with Sly the drunkard at all but by the end of Induction 2 the audience is more or less coerced into identifying with Sly: the play performed for his education and entertainment is also being put on for ours.

Act 1, Scene 1

Lucentio, a Pisan brought up in Florence, and his servant Tranio arrive in Padua; Lucentio plans to enrol at the university.

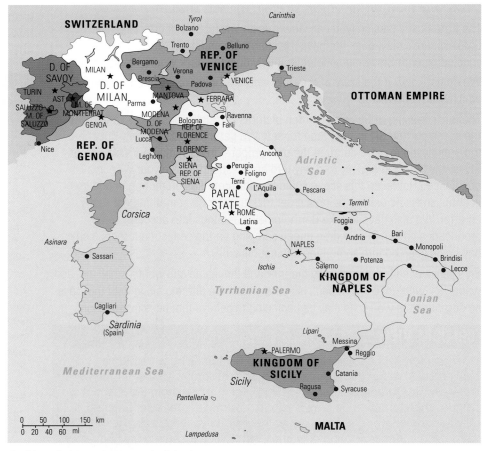

▲ Map of sixteenth-century Italian city states

Context

The Italian city states emerged from feudalism before the rest of Europe and had much higher rates of literacy and numeracy. Financial skills like banking, book-keeping and accounting became prominent. The population was more urbanised, educated and sophisticated than elsewhere. Money and commerce linked to population growth, building projects and responsive government were hallmarks of these societies, hence many historians refer to them as early or proto capitalist.

Lucentio and Tranio observe Baptista Minola, a rich Paduan merchant, enter with his two daughters, Katherine and the younger Bianca. Attending the family are Gremio and Hortensio, both suitors to Bianca.

Baptista rejects both suitors because Katherine must be married before he will allow Bianca to be courted:

> **For how I firmly am resolved you know:**
>
> **That is, not to bestow my youngest daughter**
>
> **Before I have a husband for the elder**.

Top ten quotation

It appears that Katherine is sharp-tongued and acerbic as she harangues Baptista and threatens Hortensio with violence. Lucentio compares Bianca to the goddess Minerva. Baptista asks Gremio and Hortensio if they know any 'schoolmasters' who will tutor his daughters. Gremio and Hortensio agree to collaborate to find Katherine a husband to remove the obstacle to their courting Bianca. Lucentio and Tranio devise a plan to disguise Lucentio as a schoolmaster and thereby infiltrate the Minola household: Tranio declares:

> **You will be schoolmaster**
>
> **And undertake the teaching of the maid**.

Top ten quotation

Tranio reminds his master he is in Padua to attend university and live the life of a rich young gentleman. Master and servant therefore exchange clothes. Biondello, Lucentio's other servant, arrives and is confused when he sees Tranio in his master's finery. Lucentio explains that Tranio must impersonate him because Lucentio has killed a man since arriving in Padua and is a fugitive from justice. The scene concludes with Sly claiming the play so far is 'excellent' but 'Would 'twere done'.

Build critical skills

Minerva was the Roman goddess of wisdom: Lucentio's comparison of Bianca to Minerva is ironic. Bianca may well be wise in the sense that she keeps her own counsel and makes herself look placid in contrast to her allegedly 'mad' sister. What do you think is to be gained or lost by Bianca appearing to be obedient and virtuous in public?

Commentary: Lucentio, cast here by Shakespeare as an onlooker of an almost voyeuristic nature, falls in love at first sight in a manner typical of the courtly love tradition. Also typical and predictable is his hyperbolic reaction to Bianca's supposed qualities of 'mild behaviour and sobriety'. Lucentio claims he will 'burn', 'pine' and 'perish' if he does not 'achieve' her. The meaning here is clearly sexual, no matter which way Lucentio dresses it up in courtly clothes. Though it may not be immediately obvious, the audience quickly learns that Bianca is only playing the part of the obedient child. Tranio is vital to the plot: he initiates the chain of thought which results in the plan for he and Lucentio to exchange identities. Does Lucentio decide to tell Biondello that he is in disguise because he has killed someone and is a fugitive because he wants to pretend there is a dangerous side to his nature? Lucentio can often appear to be slightly pathetic. Strangely Biondello never questions the story.

Taking it further ▶

Research Sancho Panza from Cervantes' *Don Quixote*; Mosca in Ben Jonson's play *Volpone*, Samwise Gamgee in J.R.R. Tolkien's *The Lord of the Rings*, Sam Weller of Charles Dickens' *The Posthumous Papers of the Pickwick Club* and Jeeves, Bertie Wooster's valet in P.G. Wodehouse's novels. In many ways Tranio plays the part of a sixteenth-century Jeeves against his Lucentio's Bertie Wooster.

In this scene Katherine only speaks 12 lines

Katherine is certainly vocal in her opening appearance, shockingly accusing Baptista of making a 'stale' (prostitute) of her among Gremio and Hortensio who claim she is 'too rough', a 'devil' and a 'fiend from hell'. Such cruel, diabolical imagery goes some way to explaining Katherine's antipathy towards her male neighbours – illustrated through her threats to smash a stool over Hortensio's head and 'paint' his face by tearing it with her nails. Katherine clearly has a witch-like reputation. From the sidelines Tranio claims Katherine is 'stark mad or wonderful froward'; Katherine is literally criticised from all sides. Though she feels Baptista's supposed insult very keenly, Katherine may actually be wrong: Baptista has told Bianca's suitors that she cannot be married until Katherine is married first, stating that *if* Hortensio and Gremio are interested in wooing Katherine, they have his permission. The conditional clause centred around the word 'if' is important.

Neither man is interested in wooing Katherine who, despite the invective aimed at her, says comparatively little to deserve the insults thrown at her: in this scene she speaks only 12 lines. Her detractors have far more to say about her than she has either to say to them or about herself, suggesting perhaps that the male characters whether Paduan or from further afield assume the power to define females.

However, Katherine's few lines still give a very clear indication that she is far from the Elizabethan ideal of the silent, meek, affable woman. Her verbal assault on Hortensio indicates not only her spirit but – more importantly – her propensity for violence.

Does Katherine threaten all men or merely her neighbours? She is clearly discontent with her social and familial position in relation to Bianca and is unwanted and unvalued as a prospective partner in the eyes of the rest of Paduan society. It must irk her that Bianca is considered to be more desirable. From Katherine's vantage point she is in a degrading situation, particularly as this scene is carried out in a public street where their actions can be seen by others. It may appear that Baptista favours Bianca, who is careful to make a public demonstration that 'humbly I subscribe' to his pleasure. However, it could also be argued that by Baptista needing to have a private conversation with Bianca that he has more fatherly work to do with Bianca than he does with Katherine, who as a mature adult can be allowed to please herself about whether she comes or goes. The quality and values of the production will bring out nuances of the script which may be overlooked in reading.

CRITICAL VIEW

Rebecca Warren (York Notes Advanced, 2005) interprets Baptista's words 'You may stay' to Katherine as an 'instruction' to stay outside when he goes to talk to Bianca; however, it is equally likely that he is allowing Katherine to make up her own mind about what she does. That she interprets her father's words as an insulting slight tells us a great deal about Katherine's state of mind at this point of the play. She is clearly unhappy and may misunderstand others' actions and words.

Despite the amusing and shallow romantic musings of Lucentio, marriage in this opening scene is firmly linked to finance. Gremio wonders whether it is likely that anyone will be fool enough to want to marry Katherine despite her father being 'very rich', perhaps revealing that in Paduan society marriage is part of a financial game, played by men for some gain of their own; but this is not the only analysis. Gremio is prepared later in the play to enter an auction to win Bianca's hand in marriage: he will lose money by this arrangement, not gain from it. Gremio claims that it would be beneficial to all (except Katherine?) to find someone who would 'thoroughly woo her, wed her, and bed her, and rid the house of her'. The imagery is telling: he wishes for Katherine a sort of exile following a hasty marriage. Gremio's words foreshadow Petruchio's later behaviour as he will woo her, wed her and bed her, though will do so enthusiastically. Bianca is clearly viewed in monetary terms as 'treasure' (so too is Juliet in *Romeo and Juliet*). Women as well as men saw each other's value in financial terms. Fathers had to finance any dowries that followed their daughters into a marriage. It will be Bianca and Katherine who will be in a position to benefit financially from their wedding arrangements. The financial world of the play is complex for modern audiences and cannot be explained away with generalisations. Successful students will need to make a concerted effort to understand its implications, nuances and ramifications.

Other foreshadowing occurs with the military language used to describe 'rough' Katherine who is given to 'loud 'larums', which is replicated later by Petruchio. Already we may detect that Katherine and Petruchio will have much in common.

Already we may detect that Katherine and Petruchio will have much in common

Act 1, Scene 2

Petruchio and his servant Grumio enter; Petruchio, from Verona, is seeking to add to his fortune while seeing the world following his father's death. Following some farcical horseplay with Grumio about knocking on doors and heads, Petruchio gives old friend Hortensio an account of his recent life, claiming he would like to 'wive and thrive' as best he may. Hortensio mentions Katherine who is ill-favoured but 'very rich'. Petruchio announces he will 'board' Katherine despite her roughness and reputation for being 'curst', claiming he will not sleep until he sees her. As Petruchio prepares to visit Baptista, Hortensio reveals his love for Bianca and explains Baptista's ruling that Katherine must be married before Bianca can have suitors. Hortensio asks Petruchio to offer him in disguise as a music tutor to Bianca so that he might 'unsuspected court her'.

Gremio arrives with Lucentio (disguised as schoolmaster Cambio). In offering a tutor to Baptista, Gremio wants Lucentio/Cambio to praise him so Bianca will favour him. Hortensio informs Gremio that Petruchio will woo Katherine if her dowry is sufficient. Petruchio, undaunted by the tales of Katherine's shrewish nature, asserts that he will win her easily:

Top ten quotation

> **Have I not in my time heard lions roar?**
>
> **Have I not heard the sea, puffed up with winds,**
>
> **Rage like an angry boar chafed with sweat?**

Tranio, now disguised as Lucentio, appears with Biondello and informs Gremio and Hortensio that he too will woo Bianca. The scene ends with everyone going to celebrate their good fortune that Petruchio has arrived to woo Katherine so that Bianca can be 'free' to meet her suitors.

Commentary: That Petruchio gets involved in the horseplay with Grumio is often cited that he is at heart a violent man ready to wring ears and bludgeon heads – much like Katherine in fact. Yet this is knockabout violence of the sort seen in 'custard pie comedies' of the silent film era. Directors who wish to give Petruchio many layers of psychological depth make much of his father's recent death and some productions may even portray him wearing a black armband or some other outward symbol of grief.

Petruchio seems genuinely intrigued by Katherine: he has heard that she is an 'irksome, brawling scold' but qualifies this knowledge of her nature by going on to say, if that is all she is, he hears 'no harm', implying that Katherine's faults are minor and, in the great scheme of things, inconsequential. Hortensio has described Katherine's shrewish nature as so troublesome that he 'would not wed her for a mine of gold'. Though Petruchio is interested in the gold and in that regard is very like the Paduans and the Elizabethans for whom Shakespeare, a man with a keen eye for monetary gain himself, wrote the play, the playwright clearly creates Petruchio to be an altogether more dynamic character than the men we have seen up to now. That he is so excited by the prospect of meeting the intriguing Katherine that he 'will not sleep' until he sees her shows the audience that he is prepared to undergo physical privations and emotional hardship to attain her – a theme Katherine comes back to herself in Act 5, Scene 2.

Grumio knows his master will be a match for Katherine, believing that her 'scolding would do little good upon him', acknowledging his superiority over other men who would be cowed by what in the world of the experienced Petruchio is little more than background noise. Grumio perhaps gives a hint of Petruchio's age in this scene in the phrase 'two-and-thirty, a pip out'.

CRITICAL VIEW

The 1967 Franco Zeffirelli film starring Richard Burton shows Petruchio as a drunk who makes his bold claims about being undaunted by a woman's tongue while under the influence of alcohol. In this production Petruchio is scared of Katherine's reputation and much of the comedy revolves around Petruchio plucking up sufficient courage to undertake his wooing of a Katherine who is clearly a wildcat.

Context

All over Europe the card game '31' from the French *Trente-et-un* was popular. The aim of the game was to hold cards whose 'pips', the spots on each card, added up to 31. Grumio's description of Petruchio as a 'pip out' could be a joke that his master has 'gone bust' and therefore gone a bit mad. Even if we take this interpretation, it sets up an interesting comparison, for by now both Katherine and Petruchio have been called 'mad' by other characters.

If Petruchio has turned 32 it introduces another idea into the play: comedies are usually a battle of wits between the young and the old but Petruchio and Katherine may be at that intermediate level between the extreme age of Gremio and Baptista and the extreme youth of Lucentio and Bianca. In this sense, as in many other senses in *The Taming of the Shrew,* Katherine and Petruchio are a pair of well-matched misfits.

Lucentio's appearance as Cambio and Tranio's appearance as Lucentio further the disguise motif and add extra layers to the appearance versus reality theme Shakespeare has been developing since the Induction. Petruchio's dominance over the other men is also clearly demonstrated when he threatens Tranio/Lucentio that he is not to woo Katherine. Bianca is fair game but not Katherine: 'Sir, the first's for me.' That he uses the term 'first' to describe Katherine proves her primacy in Petruchio's eyes. He is hardly aware of the outwardly conventional Bianca's existence until the final scene.

> Katherine and Petruchio are a pair of well-matched misfits

Act 2, Scene 1

In the most action-packed and complex scene in the play, the audience sees what happens behind closed doors when Katherine enters dragging her tied-up sister around the stage by the wrists. Katherine interrogates Bianca about her favourite suitor: Hortensio or Gremio? Bianca seems to be genuinely frightened by her sister's violence. Baptista separates the feuding sisters but Katherine still 'flies after Bianca', intent on more vengeful violence.

Gremio, Lucentio/Cambio, Petruchio, Hortensio/Licio, Tranio/Lucentio and Biondello enter. Petruchio announces his intention to marry Katherine and presents Hortensio as a music and mathematics tutor to Baptista's daughters. Baptista accepts 'Licio' immediately and Gremio quickly advances his man 'Cambio' as a Greek and Latin tutor. Tranio/Lucentio then announces himself as a suitor for Bianca, giving a set of books and a lute as tokens of his intent. The supposed tutors are taken inside to begin their work. Petruchio jumps straight into the arrangements of dowries and the marriage contract but Baptista insists that first Petruchio must get Katherine's love. Hortensio re-enters with his lute broken over his head, courtesy of the still violent Katherine who did not like her lesson. When Katherine arrives, Petruchio repeatedly puns on the name 'Kate', informing her 'Myself am moved to woo thee for my wife'.

TASK

A cate was an Elizabethan delicacy. In referring to Katherine as a 'cate', how far do you think Petruchio is deliberately attempting to belittle Katherine by calling her the equivalent of a modern-day term like 'sweetie'? Is it possible that he is referring to her this way to suggest that her forbidding outward demeanour is a type of disguise but that her true nature is agreeable?

Top ten quotation

Top ten quotation

The meeting is uproarious and, as the opening negotiation in a marriage match, highly unusual. Petruchio's repeated punning on the word 'Kate' gives way to sexual puns and Katherine responds in kind. During their badinage she hits him after he makes a joke about having his **'tongue'** in her **'tail'** and he threatens to 'cuff' her if she hits him again. Upon Baptista's re-entrance Petruchio announces the wedding will be on Sunday. Baptista agrees to the match despite Katherine's claims that Baptista has agreed to marry her to a **'half lunatic, a madcap ruffian'** and Petruchio exits, claiming he is going to Venice to buy things for the wedding.

Baptista turns his attention to Bianca's suitors. Gremio and Tranio vie for Bianca by telling Baptista what they will offer: whatever Gremio offers, Tranio offers more until Baptista accepts Tranio's offer, provided he can prove that he is the son of the rich Vincentio as he claims. Tranio now realises that he must get someone to impersonate his father in order to continue the masquerade and win Bianca for his master.

Commentary: This is the most important scene in the play. Its opening is both vital and controversial and the entire reception of any production can depend upon its success in the theatre: should the director play Katherine's abuse of Bianca in the same knockabout farcical style as Petruchio's and Grumio's 'knock me here' scene just witnessed or should it have an altogether darker undercurrent? Given that Katherine has bound Bianca's hands and is violently dragging her about, the scene is almost impossible to play 'just for laughs': the violence is premeditated. One cannot tie up someone else by accident: is Katherine's violent behaviour therefore a sign of a genuinely shrewish nature, which would prove Hortensio's and Gremio's analysis of her at least partially accurate? Is it a symptom of a troubled and disordered mind brought about by living in a dismissive, alienating patriarchy? Has her domestic environment where she has been overlooked, pushed out by her father's favourite Bianca, brought her to this? Is Katherine's intense interest in which of Bianca's suitors she favours a subconscious desire to be herself married? Katherine is certainly concerned that she will be publicly humiliated – a fear she acknowledges more than once in the play – and, despite everything Baptista has said and done up to now, she still seems firmly to cling to the mistaken belief that Baptista will allow Bianca to marry before she does, bitterly remonstrating with her father: 'I must dance barefoot on her wedding day / And, for your love to her, lead apes in hell.'

Context

In English folklore there was a tradition that unmarried women were supposed to dance barefoot on their sister's wedding day and a linked tradition put forward the notion that on Judgement Day the 'old maids' would lead apes into hell because they had no children to lead them into heaven. Katherine fears that her father favours Bianca and that she herself will die a virgin. Katherine's language reveals her deep insecurities.

Most directors make Baptista's speech 'Poor girl, she weeps' about Bianca, indicating Baptista's preference for his younger daughter, but it is entirely possible to see it as sympathy directed to Katherine who is weeping with frustration and that the next half line 'Go, ply thy needle' is directed at Bianca before he returns to berate Katherine. This interpretation would reveal Baptista as more even-handed than most critics acknowledge and that he is endeavouring to keep a type of equality in his dealings with his daughters. His rebuke that Katherine is a 'hilding' (a horse, or a worthless, contemptible person, usually female in Shakespeare) is cruel but perhaps no more so than Katherine's original actions in torturing and abusing her sister. Bianca's 'silence' may not be occasioned by fear alone but can be interpreted as a sign of her narcissistic and superior smugness which we have already seen in the line 'So well I know my duty to my elders'.

Bianca clearly enjoys malevolently reminding her sister of their age gap. A good production will bring out the subtle nuances of sibling rivalry and, though such grace-notes in performance cannot justify Katherine's violence, they may allow the audience to see it with more depth of context.

Following Katherine's orchestrated violence, Petruchio's inquiry to Baptista, 'Pray, have you not a daughter / Called Katherina, fair and virtuous?' is a huge signifier of Shakespeare's comic intentions as he creates suspense and excitement prior to the couple's first meeting. Baptista's response, 'I have a daughter, sir, called Katherina' is drily comic in that he cannot acknowledge Katherine's fairness and virtue especially after the violence he has just witnessed but the serious point here is that finally in Padua we have someone who is prepared to describe Katherine in glowing terms to her father, even if the reference is framed by a joke. Petruchio thus continues to disrupt and subvert others' expectations of Katherine by being prepared to acknowledge her hidden potential. Petruchio is disruptive in other ways: from the outset he has confounded others' opinions of Katherine, praising her 'beauty', 'wit', 'affability', 'modesty', and her 'wondrous qualities' and, in an echo of the praise Lucentio heaped on Bianca upon first seeing her, acknowledging her 'mild behaviour'. When Petruchio says (either in an aside, which makes it true, or to the other characters, which would make it more open to interpretation) that after her assault on Hortensio he loves this 'lusty wench' ten times more than he did before, the audience may begin to believe that he finds her spirit — similar to his own — to be genuinely attractive. Petruchio talks about Katherine very much as his social and emotional equal here and elsewhere.

In his first soliloquy Petruchio reveals that he will reverse everything Katherine does so that, for example, 'if she rail, why then I'll tell her plain / She sings as sweetly as a nightingale'.

Clearly Petruchio is seeking to confound Katherine as he has been confounding everyone else but the tactic is designed to show Katherine that whatever behaviour she displays at any given time can be replaced by a different mode of behaviour. She can transmute. Whatever she is thinking can be unravelled and recast as something else; whatever she believes about herself can be

> Bianca's silence can be interpreted as a sign of her narcissistic smugness

Context

Soliloquy is a dramatic convention where a character alone on stage reveals the true nature of their thoughts at this particular point in the play. The word derives from the Latin roots, *solus* 'alone' and *loqui* 'speak' meaning 'a talking to oneself'.

15

reconsidered and rearranged. Shakespeare's genius is in plain view here: comedy seeks to make us recast dangerous or extreme behaviours and modify them for our own good and the good of those around us. The playwright makes Petruchio his King of Comedy, around whom not only many of the comic moments but also most of the comic ideas revolve.

Build critical skills

The word 'say' appears five times in Petruchio's soliloquy and there are eight other verbs which reference speaking. In the scene as a whole Katherine resorts to violence on at least five separate occasions. Based on this analysis, what do you think Shakespeare is telling his audience about the relationship between words and violence?

CRITICAL VIEW

John Cleese performing in Jonathan Miller's 1980 BBC TV Shakespeare production speaks Petruchio's soliloquy as though he is thoughtfully making up his plan on the spot; Richard Burton in the 1967 film portrays nervousness and anxiety as he runs through his plans whereas Simon Paisley Day in the 2012 Globe production reels off what he will do as though he has already planned everything beforehand. Different interpretations reveal different sides to Petruchio's character.

The 'auction' for Bianca is important. Not only does it allow Shakespeare to show a different and far less personal type of courtship to the sort conducted by Petruchio and Katherine but it also enables the audience to get a full flavour of just how important money is in this society. However, we may logically ask, 'Where is Hortensio at this moment?' Either he has been overlooked by the playwright in an error or there are other reasons for his non-participation. Does Baptista already know that he is not as financially solvent as Gremio and the wealthy young stranger 'Lucentio' so has been deliberately excluded or is he off somewhere furtively trying to woo Bianca?

Act 3, Scene 1

Shakespeare now shifts the audience's attention to Bianca, Lucentio and Hortensio. Both men compete for Bianca's attention, trying to get Bianca alone first. Bianca resolves the dispute, telling Hortensio that while he tunes his instrument she shall study with Lucentio.

While pretending to study a Latin text Lucentio confesses his love for Bianca. She playfully rebukes him at first, saying she doesn't trust him but admitting he should 'despair not'. When Hortensio gets his chance to be alone with Bianca she is far less receptive to his advances. When Bianca is called away to help prepare for Katherine's wedding, Lucentio goes with her. Hortensio begins to realise that 'Cambio' is in love with Bianca and vows that if Bianca directs her love to Cambio he will find another woman.

Commentary: As Bianca, the supposed 'patroness of heavenly harmony', settles the infantile dispute between the pretend tutors, we hear an echo of Katherine's petulance in her claim that she 'will not be tied to hours' or 'pointed times' but will please herself. Katherine said much the same thing in Act 1, Scene 1, and will go on to say she will please herself twice in Act 3, Scene 2, and once in Act 4, Scene 3. However, after Act 4, Scene 3, Katherine turns her attention to pleasing Petruchio. From here to the end of the play all Bianca will do is essentially please herself. She clearly dominates both Hortensio and Lucentio and is certainly not the goddess Lucentio thought he saw in Act 1, Scene 1. It is ironic that both suitors try to win Bianca's favour by utilising the traditional courtly graces afforded by poetry and music. Lucentio makes use of Ovid – the Roman master of love poetry and seduction – whereas the hapless Hortensio cannot even manage to 'tune his instrument' correctly, thus symbolising his sexual inadequacy and general haplessness. Hortensio is such a flop in all walks of life that we wonder how he and the masculine Petruchio ever became friends in the first place. Hortensio's suspicions that Bianca favours Cambio are well founded but he reveals his essential shallowness by asserting that if Bianca does not favour him he will cope with his disappointment by 'changing' his love for Bianca for a love with someone else.

Act 3, Scene 2

It is the day of the wedding and the guests await Petruchio's arrival with increasing unease; Katherine, believing that Petruchio's lateness is a sign that she is about to be jilted, refuses to be humiliated publicly and leaves. Biondello announces Petruchio is on his way riding a disease-riddled horse and dressed bizarrely, accompanied by Grumio also inappropriately garbed. When Petruchio finally arrives, Baptista and Tranio implore him to change into more suitable attire but Petruchio is adamant he will not change. Everyone is invited to the church but Lucentio and Tranio remain behind, discussing their need to find someone willing to take on the role of Lucentio's father, Vincentio. Lucentio mentions his plan to marry Bianca in secret – a further deception of Baptista and his hospitality. Gremio enters with the news of the commotion at the church: Petruchio has eccentrically guzzled large quantities of altar wine, smacked the priest, flung wine sops into the sexton's face and kissed Katherine with a clamorous smack. During this performance Katherine 'trembled and shook'. The wedding party arrives from church and Petruchio declares that the wedding feast shall take place but that the guests must eat without the bride and groom. Katherine is furious, demanding that they stay, but Petruchio will not hear of it, claiming he will leave taking all of his possessions, including Katherine, with him. The newly-weds leave in an uproar and the guests show their bewilderment, most expressing the view that Petruchio is 'mad'; Bianca's view is that since Kate is mad herself she is well-matched in her new husband. The remaining guests go to the banquet with Bianca taking Katherine's place at the feast.

Commentary: Shakespeare furthers the theme of disruption here: not only does he insert a wedding – usually the climax to a comedy – in the middle of the play but he also makes it one of the funniest and zaniest in stage history. Petruchio's earlier haste in wooing and arranging the marriage is reversed as he deliberately stage-manages his own late entrance. Katherine's reaction is most revealing: though Baptista is conscious that Petruchio's lateness is making a 'mockery' of a serious ceremonial occasion, Katherine understands that if her bridegroom does not attend there will be **'no shame but mine'**. Thus the audience sees Katherine's human side and may feel some genuine sympathy

> Top ten quotation

for her, particularly when Baptista comments that Petruchio's behaviour would 'vex a saint, much more a shrew' of her 'impatient humour'. Katherine, even when she is meek and quiet, cannot shake off her shrewish image. However, she seems to inhabit a new emotional space in this scene and we see a thoughtful side not witnessed before: when she reflects on what Petruchio's lateness means she decides that not only is she being coerced into marriage against her true will, but that her prospective husband is a 'mad-brained rudesby full of spleen' who in the words reminiscent of the old folk song does not intend to wed where he hath wooed.

When Tranio tries to defend Petruchio's behaviour in declaring that he knows him well and is sure he will arrive soon, we detect a potential fault-line in the plot: how does Tranio know anything at all about a man with whom he is barely acquainted? The audience is warned of Petruchio's arrival via Biondello's highly descriptive speech, rich in visual imagery describing mismatched and inappropriate clothing and horse diseases, so in the theatre the sense of comic anticipation is palpable. Petruchio's anarchic arrival is usually greeted with roars of laughter. Here is a man who genuinely does not care less what others think of him; his bullish self-confidence is remarkable. His purpose is to disrupt solemnity with absurdity, to push social conventions far beyond the limits of predictable extremism into territory completely unimagined by less sophisticated thinkers. Yet he is a rebel with a cause: he wants to demonstrate to Katherine the sort of impact her extreme behaviour has had on those around her. She has been unable or unwilling to see things from anyone's perspective other than her own and has become trapped in a world where her reactions to events have been childish, inappropriate, wrong-headed or dangerous. Petruchio's lateness, his mode of dress, his manky horse, his inappropriate conduct at the service and his insistence on crashing *out* of his own wedding feast with his newly-acquired parcel of 'goods' in the shape of Katherine signal both his mastery of the situation and his talent as a magnificent actor-manager. This is just a game but played for serious stakes: 'To me she's married, not unto my clothes.' Petruchio acts the madman so he can hold up a metaphorical mirror to Katherine in which she may recognise that her earlier behaviour was untoward, unsophisticated and a symptom of unhappiness. Petruchio will continue to act the lunatic until Katherine learns a new role.

Shakespeare advances the sub-plot during the time the principals are off stage. We detect a growing urgency in Lucentio's plan to marry Bianca secretly. Again, we see the huge gulf in behaviour and values between Petruchio and Lucentio: though it may be odd, Petruchio's behaviour up to now has always been in public, in front of an audience, conducted on an epic scale, whereas Lucentio has been skulking in corners, posing as someone else surreptitiously trying to gain a sexual advantage. Bianca's replacement of her sister at the wedding feast is literal as well as symbolic; she will be married soon, though in secret and not in public, and in her behaviour the audience will see that it is she, not Katherine, who is the real shrew.

Act 4, Scene 1

Miserable and cold, Grumio arrives at Petruchio's house ahead of his master and mistress with orders for the other servants to prepare the house. Grumio tells Curtis how the journey has been full of incident and reveals how Katherine's horse fell and she landed in the mire with the horse on top of her. Instead of rushing to Katherine's aid, Petruchio blamed Grumio and began to beat him. Tellingly, Katherine got herself out from under the horse and plucked Petruchio off Grumio. When the newly-weds enter, Petruchio shouts at the servants for failing to carry out his orders. This bullying and hectoring behaviour continues when the meal is served, with Petruchio striking the servants and throwing food about the stage. Petruchio complains that the meat is burnt and unsuitable because he and Katherine are both choleric by nature. Instead he bundles Katherine off to their bedchamber where, despite his earlier sexual promises in Act 2, Scene 1 to make himself 'warm' in her bed, he gives a 'sermon of constancy'. In soliloquy Petruchio outlines his plan to tame Katherine: in the manner of a hawk being trained by its master he will deprive her of food and sleep, insisting that **'all is done in reverend care of her'** so that he can curb her **'mad and headstrong humour'**.

> Top ten quotation

Commentary: Petruchio continues the act he began at the wedding and it is revealing that Curtis notices in his odd behaviour that 'he is more shrew than she'. Petruchio's manic behaviour is clearly out of character and Peter (Petruchio's servant) remarks 'He kills her in her own humour.'

CRITICAL VIEW

J. Dennis Huston in '"To Make a Puppet": Play and Play-Making in *The Taming of the Shrew*', *Shakespeare Studies* 9 (1976) claims that Petruchio's behaviour towards Katherine during courtship and beyond is 'nothing less than psychological rape', suggesting that Petruchio 'touches upon the 'low, the bestial, in man's nature'. However, Robert Heilman in 'The Taming Untamed; or The Return of the Shrew', *Modern Language Quarterly* 27 (1966), calls Petruchio a 'remarkable therapist'.

Grumio's speech to Curtis offers evidence that a plan has been hatched between himself and Petruchio in the matter of Katherine's treatment. Grumio was also clearly an 'insider' in the business of the crazy costuming and mock-frantic exit from the wedding. Part of the plan is to find fault with the food and thereby starve Katherine into a state of submission. Grumio has, no doubt, also been 'set up' for the comedy cuffing he received when Katherine's horse fell. Some critics make the point that somehow Petruchio made Katherine's horse fall but this seems far-fetched when we examine the folklore traditions which prompted much of the play (see 'The oral tradition' in the **Contexts** section on p. 58). In the oral tradition the woman either rides on the back of the husband's horse – hence Curtis' curiosity on the subject – or she walks while her husband rides.

Shakespeare's Petruchio gives Katherine her own horse and she falls by herself. That he symbolically waits for her to extricate herself is, perhaps, evidence that Katherine's recovery will need to be as much brought about by her own efforts as by Petruchio's behaviour.

Has Katherine's spirit already been broken as is often argued? Perhaps. She says very little but is cold, hungry, tired and splattered with mud. Would anyone be talkative in such circumstances? In the same way that while in Padua she occasionally used the formal 'sir' when addressing her father, she addresses Petruchio with a formal 'you' rather than the more familiar 'thou' derived from '*tu*', the 'you' singular in French. Significantly Katherine can now empathise with others, asking Petruchio to forgive the servants for burning the meat as it was 'a fault unwilling'. In public Petruchio maintains the act of behaving like a domestic tyrant but in his concluding soliloquy we observe more of the same sort of philosophising he used before he met Katherine for the first time: he is in no doubt of his own supremacy as he uses the term 'my reign' and it is obvious that he views the taming of his wife to be an essential ingredient in the achievement of happiness for them both. At this stage the shrew imagery scattered throughout the first of half of the play is replaced by a particularly dense cluster of hawking images. (See the **Extended commentary** on this scene on p. 88.)

Taking it further ▶

Research Elizabethan ideas about madness and apply them to the behaviour of Katherine and Petruchio in the play.

Act 4, Scene 2

Tranio and Hortensio spy on how Bianca behaves when in the company of Lucentio, who woos his student by mentioning Ovid's *Art of Love*.

Context

Roman poet Ovid's *Ars Amatoria* (Art of Love) was a part tongue-in-cheek, part serious, three-part guide to male-female relationships. Book one tells a man the best ways to get a woman; book two gives him advice on how to keep her. The third book gives women advice on first how to win and then how to keep a man. Often accused of vulgarity (it offers women advice on the best sexual positions to adopt depending on age and body shape) it was massively popular.

Tranio feigns outrage at the inconstancy of woman in line 14 and Hortensio reveals his identity, agreeing that he will forswear (agree to give up or do without) Bianca. He reveals that in three days' time he will marry a wealthy widow who has loved him as long as he has loved Bianca. When he leaves, Tranio tells Bianca and Lucentio what has happened and that 'Licio' is no longer a suitor. As they rejoice Biondello appears with the news that he has found an old man suitable to play the role of Vincentio. (This character is either a pedant – a teacher – or merchant, depending upon the edition. Here we refer to him as pedant.) The stranger from Mantua is duped by Tranio who persuades him that he is in danger in Padua because there is a feud between the dukes of the two city states. Fearful that he might be executed, the pedant agrees to impersonate Vincentio and to give assurances to Baptista about Lucentio's wealth and status.

Commentary: In this scene Shakespeare returns to the sub-plot where we see yet another example of characters spying on others unobserved. We have seen it in Act 1, Scene 1 when Lucentio and Tranio observed Baptista, his daughters and Bianca's suitors and will see it again in Act 5, Scene 1 when Petruchio and Katherine observe the unravelling of the disguise plot. Tranio encourages Hortensio to see the worst in Bianca via the phrase 'See how beastly she doth court him', thus enabling the audience simultaneously to recognise Tranio's skill as Lucentio's agent and to get another glimpse into Bianca's true nature. Though perhaps not 'beastly' (she does not get insensibly drunk like Sly) we can see how much power she has. The audience also recognises that the animal insults aimed at Katherine, the alleged 'shrew', are now being used against Bianca, thus marking a change from Bianca's imagined perfection to something more worldly. Hortensio's speed in abandoning Bianca is a sign that his attachment was shallow all along. Biondello's news that he has found someone to impersonate Vincentio keeps the notion of disguise and deception in front of the audience as Shakespeare prepares for the climax of his 'disguises' sub-plot. Tranio works yet another of his believable subterfuges by persuading the pedant that there is an inter-city war between Padua and Mantua and therefore the disguise as Vincentio will save his life. Yet again, we see that in the sub-plot the servant is cleverer than the master.

Act 4, Scene 3

Deprived of sleep, hungry Katherine begs Grumio to bring some food. He teases her with offers of delicacies but does not give her anything on the grounds that the foods are choleric. The stage directions show that she beats him for tormenting her. Petruchio appears with Hortensio bearing food for Katherine which Petruchio says he has prepared himself. When her thanks are not immediately forthcoming Petruchio removes the dish and in an aside tells Hortensio to eat it all. Before getting the chance to assuage her hunger, a tailor and haberdasher arrive to fit Katherine for some new clothes. Petruchio rejects the cap and gown that they have brought, ignoring Katherine's protests, who likes the garments and wishes to keep them. Petruchio satirises the tailor who defends the quality of the gown saying that he is only following instructions given by Grumio who joins the quibble to defend his own actions. The tailor is dismissed. In an aside Petruchio tells Hortensio to pay the tailor later and sets about lecturing his wife: he tells Katherine clothes and outward appearances are not important. Petruchio then announces that they will 'feast and sport' at her father's house and are to leave immediately. He deliberately mistakes the time of day, saying it is seven o'clock, and Katherine corrects him by telling him it is two o'clock: Petruchio warns her against contradicting him and the visit is cancelled.

Context

The adjective 'gorgeous' when describing female clothing is included in the words of the Elizabethan wedding ceremony, which exhort the new wife not to be overly concerned with 'gorgeous apparel', as such shallow concerns as fashion will dilute the couple's focus on 'mild and quiet' spirituality deemed as vital for a happy union.

Commentary: Katherine's admission that she has 'never needed' to 'entreat' before is an important milestone on her personal journey. This exchange and the rest of the scene present ideas about what is necessary and what is merely desirable in life. Shakespeare begins with food and moves onto clothing which has more status-importance. Katherine's violence against Grumio is the last she will perpetrate in the play and is usually presented farcically, further to illustrate her transmutation from dangerous wildcat to someone suited to Petruchio in beliefs and behaviour. In many productions the violence is deliberately reminiscent of Petruchio's knockabout violence with Grumio in Act 1, Scene 1.

Petruchio wants Katherine to learn how to distinguish between what she needs and what she merely wants. When she learns to be 'gentle' – i.e. when she shows gratitude for services and kindnesses – she can have luxuries such as clothing suited to the 'fashion of the time'.

In the sixteenth century, gifts were exchanged frequently at different stages of courtship but we do not see this in the play after gifts from Tranio and Lucentio of books and a lute in Act 2, Scene 1 due to the haste in which the marriages are arranged. The gifts that Petruchio arranges to give Katherine *after* the marriage are culturally significant. Of particular interest is the idea of Katherine's cap which we see here but which 'becomes her not' in Act 5, Scene 2. The cap can be seen as symbolic of their relationship in terms of its values; 1 Corinthians 11:5 says, 'Every woman who prays or prophesies with her head uncovered dishonours her head, for that is one and the same as if her head were shaved.' Christian women therefore covered their heads not only in church, but also any time they were in public.

Context

The word 'milliner', a maker of women's hats, was first recorded in 1529 when the term referred to the products for which Milan and the northern Italian regions were well known. The haberdashers who imported these fashionable items came to be known as 'Millaners' from which the word was eventually derived.

Puritan Philip Stubbes, as well as attacking actors in *The Anatomy of Abuses* (1583), wrote coruscating condemnations of women's fashions. He didn't like tailors who 'do nothing else but invent new fashions, disguised shapes, and monstrous forms of apparel every day'. He hated modern hats: 'Sometimes they (women) wear them sharp on the crown, perking up like a sphere, or shaft of a steeple, standing a quarter of a yard above the crown of their heads … other ornaments (are worn) such, as French hood, hat, cap … some of this fashion, some of that, and some of this colour, some of that, according to the variable fantasies of their serpentine minds … So far hath this canker of pride eaten into the body of the common wealth, that every poor Yeoman's Daughter, every Husbandman's daughter, & every Cottager's Daughter, will not spare to flaunt it out in such gowns, whereby it cometh to pass that one can scarcely know who is a noble woman, who is an honourable or worshipful Woman, from them of the meaner sort.' Stubbes seems to hate just about everything: the theatre; actors; tailors; dressmakers and haberdashers; women's fashions; women themselves for their 'serpentine minds'; emerging notions of equality. Shakespeare has enormous fun describing what the clothes made for Katherine might look like to a Puritan of Stubbes' self-righteous biliousness. Yes, let's laugh at the anti-theatre, anti-female, anti-life Puritans, but there is also a serious point here too (see section on 'Disguises, supposes, exchanges and clothing' in **Themes**). Finery is desirable but ''tis the mind that makes the body rich'.

Petruchio's psychotherapy regime for Katherine (or misogynistic cruelty, as you prefer) is continued with his peremptory cancellation of the trip to Baptista's due to Katherine arguing about the time. His comment 'It shall be what o clock I say it is' indicates either that Katherine is the victim of mindless bullying or that Petruchio is inviting Katherine to share his anarchic and 'madcap' world view where concepts like time do not matter.

Act 4, Scene 4

Tranio and the pedant arrive at Baptista's house. When Baptista enters with Lucentio, Tranio introduces the pedant as his father Vincentio come to vouch for him. The pedant confirms the dowry Tranio has offered, confirming he has no objection to the marriage between Lucentio and Bianca. However, Baptista does not wish to draw up the wedding agreement in his own home because Gremio, who is still in the vicinity, may interrupt them. Baptista agrees to go to Lucentio's lodgings to complete the transaction and sends Lucentio (whom Baptista still thinks is Cambio) to inform Bianca that she is to become Lucentio's wife. When Tranio leaves with Baptista, Biondello returns with Lucentio and explains to his master that, instead of taking Bianca to an engagement supper later that evening, he needs to take her to St Luke's church to conduct his secret marriage.

Commentary: This scene marks the height of the Supposes (disguises) part of the plot, making the audience ask very serious questions about appearance and reality in a similar way to the questions asked in the main Petruchio–Katherine plot and in the Induction. The servants in the sub-plot continue to be better organised than Lucentio: Tranio arranges the deception of Baptista by introducing him to the supposed Vincentio so perfectly that Baptista has no qualms in agreeing to the match. Biondello comes into his own as an organiser too, explaining to his master the arrangements for the secret marriage and having to chivvy along the increasingly twittish Lucentio to make haste. Importantly, the audience will notice the irony in Baptista's statement that Bianca and 'Lucentio' are clearly so in love 'Or both dissemble deeply their affections'. Baptista has been hoodwinked by just about everyone. Lucentio's, Tranio's, Hortensio's and the pedant's disguises have all worked; but most importantly Baptista has been deceived by Bianca who has only ever been pretending to be a compliant and obedient daughter.

Context

For theatre to work it requires the 'willing suspension of disbelief', therefore it is a theatrical convention that disguises, no matter how flimsy, always work. The tradition continues in the *Superman* franchise where Clark Kent's workmates never realise he is the Man of Steel.

For all of her faults while in her father's house, Katherine never hid her personality or lied about what she was thinking and feeling.

CRITICAL VIEW

Actor Janet McTeer views this scene as vital to the whole play, arguing that Katherine is not defeated here as Petruchio never intends to crush her. Her compliance is not a submission; 'her spirit is not bowed'. However, Jeanne Addison Roberts in 'Horses and Hermaphrodites: Metamorphoses in *The Taming of the Shrew*', interprets Petruchio's behaviour here as 'monstrous'.

Build critical skills

As you read this guide and other critical works, keep a record of five or six theories that have been put forward about *The Taming of the Shrew* and add a note of how different audiences over the centuries have responded to the play.

Act 4, Scene 5

Petruchio and Katherine, accompanied by Hortensio, are on their return journey to Baptista's house. Petruchio now insists that it is night time, referring to how brightly 'shines the moon'. When Katherine says that the light is created by the sun he declares that they will all turn around and return home. Katherine finally capitulates, acknowledging that she will see the world through her husband's eyes – despite the evidence of her own – and will contradict him no more. Petruchio immediately puts her to the test and greets an old man they meet on the road as if he were a beautiful young woman, urging Katherine to do the same. When she follows his instructions, Petruchio rebukes Katherine who apologises for her 'mad mistaking', brilliantly claiming that the sun had dazzled her. The old man announces that he is Vincentio on his way from Pisa to see Lucentio in Padua. Petruchio informs him that Lucentio has married Bianca and the travellers continue their journey together. Hortensio confirms the report that Lucentio and Bianca are married and, left alone on stage for a moment, reveals he is of good heart because if his widow is 'froward' he will use Petruchio's techniques to tame her.

Commentary: The audience knows that this is the second time this journey has been attempted and that the previous attempt in Act 4, Scene 3 was abandoned. Katherine's willingness to enter into the spirit of Petruchio's antics creates much critical controversy.

However, Katherine's language is playful, showing she is enjoying the joke and so the audience will be probably justified in assuming she has joined Petruchio's madcap world. How can Petruchio know of the wedding between Lucentio and Bianca when it hasn't happened yet? This is either a plot inconsistency or evidence that Petruchio, Katherine and Hortensio – who knows he has lost Bianca – assume that the wedding will have taken place because Bianca (and Baptista) will be bound to have chosen Lucentio (real or supposed) over Gremio. The scene ends with Katherine being praised as 'merry' by Vincentio who seems happy to accompany the band of friends to Padua. Symbolically Shakespeare is showing Katherine's acceptance in wider society.

Act 5, Scene 1

Lucentio goes off to marry Bianca after Biondello informs the couple that the priest is waiting. Petruchio shows Vincentio to his son's lodgings and Vincentio invites Petruchio and his party for a drink. They knock on the door; Gremio, standing in the street, encourages them to knock louder and when they do so the pedant responds. Vincentio asks the pedant to tell Lucentio his father has arrived but the pedant accuses Vincentio of lying, claiming he is Lucentio's father. Petruchio and Katherine stand aside to watch the shenanigans. When Biondello arrives from church he is recognised by Vincentio but pretends that he does not know him and Vincentio begins to beat him, creating such a fuss that the pedant, Tranio and Baptista leave the house and arrive on stage.

Vincentio, astonished when Tranio appears dressed in his son's 'pearl and gold', fears Lucentio has been murdered by his own servant. Tranio claims not to know Vincentio, accusing him of being mad, and he calls for an officer to imprison him. Gremio tries to intercede, saying he believes that the stranger is the right Vincentio but when Gremio says that Tranio is Lucentio, Baptista also calls for Vincentio to be taken away. At this moment Lucentio and Bianca arrive and Lucentio kneels begging forgiveness. Knowing the game is up, Biondello, the pedant and Tranio all run away. Baptista asks where Lucentio is, thinking that he has just seen him run off but Lucentio confesses he is 'the right Lucentio, / Right son to the right Vincentio' and explains to Baptista that he has married Bianca in secret. The fathers are not satisfied, though Vincentio is relieved his son has not been murdered and they go into the house together to 'sound the depth of this knavery', Lucentio telling his new bride that Baptista will accept the situation. Gremio, finally realising he will never have Bianca, accepts that all he has to look forward to is his share of the feast. He exits leaving Katherine and Petruchio alone on stage. Katherine urges her husband to follow the others and Petruchio asks for a kiss. When she claims to be not ashamed of her husband but ashamed of kissing in the street, Petruchio says they will go home again but Katherine, now calling Petruchio 'love', grants him a kiss before they exit to seek out the other characters.

Commentary: At only 138 lines long this deliciously comic scene replete with discoveries and excitement is a masterclass in Shakespeare's talent as a dramatist. Every line and stage direction does a job. Lucentio is aware that he may need an extra line of defence so advises Biondello to remain near his lodgings while he slips away to get married. However, Biondello does not trust his master even to get to the church on his own without mishap so tells him he will see him safely to the church and he will return to his lodgings afterwards.

Despite the comedy there is a dark undercurrent relayed to the audience via the threats of violence. Vincentio still wants to slit Tranio's nose for calling for him to be sent to jail and he beats Biondello. Petruchio and Katherine are able to stand aside peacefully and watch the confusion unfold. For once, Katherine is not in the eye of the storm, emotionally or physically.

Context

Bergamo, an inland town at the foothills of the Alps a hundred miles from the sea, may be considered inappropriate as a centre of sail-making and critics have often attacked Shakespeare's ignorance here. However, cloth-making, including sail-making, was a major industry on the northern side of the upper Po valley in medieval and early modern times. The area around Bergamo is the rainiest in Italy; this climate favours crops of flax and hemp and may help explain Vincentio's insult of 'crackhemp' aimed at Tranio.

Top ten quotation

The final physical disguises of the play are removed when Lucentio and Tranio reveal their true identities. Lucentio still speaks in hyperbolic terms when he claims **'love wrought these miracles'** but perhaps the audience isn't so easily taken in; his servants and Bianca orchestrated the wedding. Symbolically this is the end of the disguise plot and it is clear that Shakespeare shows Petruchio as doffing his 'one half lunatic' act too. Katherine seems much happier, having the confidence to suggest in line 132 that they follow the others to see the end of the altercation. She appears to have joined his alternative world. Tellingly he asks for a kiss and, despite her maidenly shyness about kissing in the street (is the officer still on stage? is Grumio still at hand?), Katherine agrees after his playful threat to go home again. Kissing is mentioned in *Shrew* as many times as it is mentioned in *Romeo and Juliet* (16 times in both plays) but this is the first time the audience witness a kiss.

Act 5, Scene 2

Lucentio welcomes the guests to the banquet held to celebrate his marriage to Bianca as well as the marriages of Hortensio to the widow and Petruchio to Katherine. There is much joking about shrewish wives and, prompted by Petruchio, the husbands place bets on which wife is 'most obedient' and will come when summoned. Biondello is despatched to summon Bianca who says she is busy and cannot come; next the widow is summoned who will not come, believing some jest to be in progress. Contrary to expectations, Katherine obeys Petruchio's summons immediately and is sent off stage to 'swinge' in Bianca and the widow. Baptista, impressed, grants Petruchio a second dowry of twenty thousand crowns because of the changes he can see in Katherine. Petruchio tells Katherine her cap is not becoming and she is to 'throw it underfoot', an instruction 'she obeys'. Petruchio then instructs Katherine to 'tell these headstrong women/ What duty they do owe their lords and husbands'. Katherine lectures the widow and Bianca on how a wife should behave, arguing that women are essentially weaker than men; she offers to place her hand beneath her husband's foot as a token of her duty. Petruchio is delighted with his wife and after another kiss whisks her off to bed.

Commentary: Petruchio disrupts what appears to be an initially harmonious scene by niggling Hortensio that he 'fears his widow'. Upon the widow's retort that 'he that is giddy thinks the world turns round', Katherine intervenes of her own free will. Is this in defence of her husband? Katherine is irritated and perhaps hurt by the widow's explanation that her husband is 'troubled with a shrew' but, rather than attacking the widow physically as she may have once done, she contents herself – for now – by acknowledging the widow's meanness. Hunting and hawking imagery is used with the phrase 'To her!' and Shakespeare, once again, has fun with sexual innuendo around 'head', 'butt', and 'horn'. Bianca shows a hitherto unseen earthy side to her nature here by making a joke about her 'bush', a double-entendre punning on archery and sex. Katherine is never this vulgar. When Petruchio hears for the second time in this scene that his wife is 'the veriest shrew of all', this time the insult given by Baptista while Katherine is off stage, he proposes the bet. Is he irritated that Katherine's earlier restraint has gone unnoticed? Shakespeare cleverly builds up the dramatic tension by the refusal of both Bianca and the widow to come. When Katherine arrives it takes everyone but Petruchio by surprise and the speech she makes is one of the most controversial in all of Shakespeare.

CRITICAL VIEW

In the most recent Arden Shakespeare edition (2014 reprint), Barbara Hodgdon provides a brilliant résumé of how Katherine's last speech has been interpreted by performers and directors in the section of the introduction entitled 'Katherina on Behalf of the Play' (pp. 118–31). It is warmly recommended.

Petruchio ordering Katherine to remove her cap may look like bullying but it is significant in terms of the Elizabethan wedding service itself. Just before the newly-married couple left the church the minister reminded them of the words of Saint Peter who himself was referring to the Old Testament: 'For after this manner (in the old time) did the holy women, which trusted in God, apparel themselves, being subject to their own husbands.' It was a reminder for women to dress in a seemly fashion approved by their husbands, a notion modern feminists would find appalling. However, when Petruchio instructs Katherine to remove the cap he is – even if he is perfectly serious and this is not part of a private joke – asking her to keep to a vow she made before she left church on her wedding day and, of course, is reminding Bianca and the widow of a vow they had made that very day. Petruchio's response to Hortensio about what Katherine's obedience 'bodes' is also liturgical and is an echo of the words from the wedding service:

> Marry, peace it bodes, and love, and quiet life,
> An awful rule, and right supremacy,
> And to be short, what not that's sweet and happy

'So that the spirit be mild and quiet' was one of the benefits of marriage, along with sex, companionship, parenting and mutual love and support.

Katherine does not recommend or advocate a male free-for-all, despite what many critics have asserted. The Elizabethan marriage was a legal agreement of two parts in which both the man and woman had responsibilities: the man's specific role was to 'love, comfort and honour' and the specific responsibilities of the wife were to 'obey, serve and love'. The arrangement was understood as a contract: in return for love, comfort and honour, the woman provided obedience, servitude and love, but mutual love is the common denominator. If the man did not provide comfort and honour, the woman was not obliged to be obedient, which was conditional. The contract revolved around the husband's 'honest' behaviour and '**honest will**', a combination of **Canon Law** and

Canon Law: the law governing the affairs of a Christian Church, especially the law created and implemented via Papal authority in the Roman Catholic Church since the time of Saint Peter, and, within the Church of England, those laws agreed in the Book of Canons approved by the Convocations of Canterbury and York in 1604 and 1606 respectively.

Top ten quotation

Common Law: the cornerstone of the English legal system where legal precedent is made by judges sitting in court. Introduced in 1189 the doctrine of legal precedent requires similar cases to be adjudicated in a like manner: each case will bind future cases on the same generic set of facts both horizontally and vertically in the court structure. The decisions of the Supreme Court are binding on every other court in the kingdom.

Common Law. If the husband upheld his part of the contract, the wife would uphold hers.

Despite Lucentio's acknowledgement that Petruchio has bettered him: 'Well, go thy ways, old lad, for thou shalt ha't' he is still petulantly resentful about Bianca as the truth about his marriage sinks in. Tranio's first description of Katherine in Act 1, Scene 1 was that she was 'wonderful froward' and now his master's final description of his erstwhile 'Minerva' is that Bianca is 'froward'. *The Taming of the Shrew* has turned full circle; by the end of a play based on the notion of disguise and mistaken identities Katherine and Bianca have effectively exchanged places.

Finally we may wonder what has become of Sly and Bartholomew: 'out there' somewhere in the mythological world of theatre, the curtain has fallen, the actors have changed out of their costumes, the audience has gone home but somehow Sly and his pretend wife are eternally watching an empty stage waiting for the next play to entertain and instruct them.

Themes

Target your thinking

- How can a thorough understanding of the play's themes extend your knowledge of the text? (**AO1**)

Disguises, supposes, exchanges and clothing

There are two main categories of disguise in the play: the emotional, for example when characters pretend to be other than they are; and the physical, when a costume and a 'supposed' identity is worn. Judging by her later behaviour, Bianca may always have been a pretender, feigning obedience and acting the role of compliant daughter in order to get her own way. It would seem that Katherine may never pretend but that Petruchio does. However, where an audience places Petruchio's pretending is moot depending upon preferences and critical theories: he could be bluffing when he says he comes to 'wive it wealthily in Padua' when in reality he is looking for someone who will be prepared to share his unusual world view. His entire larger-than-life persona may be an elaborate bluff or it may be his real self. Perhaps less difficult to pin down are Lucentio's reasons for wishing to don a physical disguise by exchanging clothes with Tranio: he wants access to Bianca and is prepared to be dishonest and devious, particularly to Baptista, in order to be successful. He may look like a harmless young gentleman but he is unscrupulous and deceitful. Tranio, who seems to be at least as good at Latin as his master, who pretends to be a Latin tutor, successfully masquerades as Lucentio for the majority of the play and swans about keeping 'house, and port, and servants' and behaving and dressing as a man of substantial means. No one doubts him. Even when Vincentio turns up it takes Lucentio's confession to reveal to the others the truth that Tranio has been a fraud.

Marxist critics find in Shakespeare's presentation of clothing a witty critique on bourgeois affectations: the tailor's gown with its sleeve like a 'demi-cannon' but 'carved like an apple tart' and the 'custard-coffin' cap all show the worthlessness of expensive luxury items that people purchase for status rather than practicality and comfort. Petruchio's crazy costume at his wedding is proof to Marxists that Shakespeare is using Petruchio to make a point about the shallowness of fashion against the importance of making meaningful human relationships: 'To me she's married not unto my clothes'. Clothes are 'baubles', as Petruchio points out in Act 5, Scene 2, and only the clever servant Tranio, masquerading as another rich man among the Paduan bourgeoisie, spots that 'he has some meaning in his mad attire'.

Courtship and marriage

Today it is more usual to marry for love than money – or as Petruchio and Katherine may appear to do – for love *and* money. In Tudor England there was the belief that there should be no great disparity in marriage matches; families and friends sought the pairing of 'like with like' not necessarily solely in economic terms, as partners would seldom come from identical financial backgrounds, but also in terms of personality, outlook and temperament. Petruchio talks about Katherine as his clear and unequivocal social and emotional equal in Act 2, Scene 1 when he explains to Baptista:

> I am as peremptory as she proud-minded,
> And where two raging fires meet together
> They do consume the thing that feeds their fury [...]
> So I to her, and so she yields to me,
> For I am rough and woo not like a babe.

Petruchio talks about Katherine very much as his social and emotional equal

Gremio has already called Katherine 'too rough' in Act 1, Scene 1 and here Petruchio identifies her similarity to his own proud-mindedness, roughness and adulthood.

The making of marriage takes place within a specific society in a specific place within the social, financial and educational constraints of a specific historical period. Marriage choices for our ancestors depended largely upon financial concerns. Diana O'Hara in *Courtship and Constraint: Rethinking the Making of Marriage in Tudor England* (University of Manchester, 2002) demonstrates clearly via her analysis of over 250 wills and parish records in Kent that even families of relatively low social status sought to provide portions or dowries to their daughters after their deaths. The Kent wills also demonstrate that hard commercial bargaining, estimates of 'worthiness', the participation of parents and the feelings of the extended families all had to be considered before a marriage was decided.

Context

Eric Carlson (*History Today* 43, 1993) shows that the age of first marriages in Shakespeare's England was comparatively late. While the average age varied from parish to parish, the national mean was 27 for men and 25 for women, within an average range of 24 to 30 for men, and 22 to 27 for women. Perhaps a reason for late marriages was economic: a couple starting a household before the establishment of regular income then, as now, may have faced poverty.

Before marrying, couples were expected to have the resources to maintain a family; resources need to be accrued. Today families have the potential of a safety net provided by the state benefits system but Elizabethan families did not. Therefore it is a safe assumption to say money and materialism were more important to Elizabethan families than to many of their modern counterparts. Petruchio arrives in Padua as very much the finished article in terms of experience – has he not in his time 'heard lions roar […] and great ordnance in the field'? His wealth is established; following his father's death, he has 'crowns in his purse and goods at home'. O'Hara's important evidence from the wills shows that the age at which parents (usually fathers) considered that their children were mature enough to make their own decisions as adults was 21 for men (the legal age of full male independence) and the late teens, usually 18 or 19, for women. Katherine's exact age is not given but she is older than Bianca. Most directors cast an actress somewhat older than 19 to play the part.

Build critical skills

◀ Sam Spiro and Simon Paisley Day in the Frow 2012 Globe production

For Toby Frow's 2012 Globe production 42-year-old Samantha Spiro (born 1968) was cast as Katherine and 43-year-old Simon Paisley Day (born 1967) was cast as Petruchio. What do you think is to be gained and lost by a production casting actors who are substantially older than those playing Lucentio and Bianca?

Katherine is certainly old enough to make her own decisions and one of the things that enrages her is when she believes she has been 'appointed hours' like a child (Act 1, Scene 1). Katherine is also not enamoured of the choice of local men. She may be waiting for the right man but, as Hortensio says, there is 'small choice in rotten apples'. Her frustrated rage may not be because she is against marriage per se but because she does not like either the choice of prospective husbands or the courtship rituals of her native Padua. O'Hara proves that in Kent courtship rituals were encouraged to take place at particular times of the year and in particular places on specific days. Couples were especially likely to meet at fairs, taverns, marketplaces, church occasions and less formal arenas like particular fields or even individual stiles, for example during harvest times. However, we have to exercise caution in our understanding and application of such historic detail. O'Hara's focus is more on the ordinary citizenry than the super-rich. What happened in Kent may not have happened in Shakespeare's native Warwickshire or cosmopolitan London; however, at least we have a sixteenth-century English template from which to base our analyses. Clearly, clusters of neighbours meeting in their own locale and forming romantic affiliations are not entirely replicated in the play. Hortensio and Gremio, as well as Katherine and Bianca, live in Padua and are clearly neighbours. Other characters are strangers: Lucentio, born in Pisa, has been brought up in Florence; Petruchio arrives from Verona but says he will purchase his wedding attire, 'rings and things' in Venice. The ineffectual Hortensio and pathetic Gremio do not make the same impression as the exciting strangers.

Money

Kathryn Hunter played Katherine at the Globe in 2003 and in an interview with the *Guardian* told of how 'rankled' she felt that her father Baptista 'was going to marry her off after a single interview'. Is this comment of 'significance'? Part of a successful student's job involves weighing up all the potential contributions to how a text can be analysed: through the way the text is constructed and written; through text-specific contexts that can be relevantly applied; through connecting the text to other texts; and then finding potential meanings and interpretations. Clearly in terms of **historicism** and critical perspective Kathryn Hunter's view *is* significant about the *Shrew* in performance and its reception in the early twenty-first century. Many modern critics, especially Marxists, see the trading of daughters for financial gain as more disturbingly misogynistic than Petruchio's 'taming' tactics. As we have seen, women took a dowry with them into marriage and many men were not above gold-digging. Indeed Petruchio claims that he is in Padua 'Haply to wive and thrive' as best he may claiming 'wealth is (the) burden of my wooing dance.' He may be lying or making fun of Paduan society but he still says it.

In Baptista's auction of Bianca, Gremio and Tranio/Lucentio do little more than list increasingly expensive sums of money and material possessions. Watching the auction is like watching a game of poker wondering which of the players

historicism: is a method of academic investigation that assigns major significance to specific contexts such as historical period, geographical location and local culture. It places great importance on the contextualised interpretation of information and rejects the notion that ideas, values and beliefs can exist independent of timeframe, place or circumstance.

will fold first. Gremio finally cracks when he has offered 'everything'; Tranio knows that Lucentio's family wealth is sufficient to cover the bid but it is a staggering amount of money which Tranio puts on the table to win Baptista's approval for his master Lucentio's marriage to Bianca. It would appear that marriage can be bought in this early capitalist society and that in this particular marriage mercantilism is more important than genuine affection. Not that Bianca appears to care. Despite her appearance of obedience to Baptista, she is happy to collude with Lucentio after he has cast aside his identity as Cambio and agrees without reservation to the secret wedding. It is a delicious irony that Shakespeare gives the super-rich Lucentio the disguise name of Cambio, which is Italian for a money exchange. In Act 5, Scene 1 Bianca seems to be aware of this meaning when in explaining the disguises states 'Cambio is changed into Lucentio'. Other than a cursory three-word apology, 'Pardon dear father', that is all she has to say on the subject of her deception and secret marriage for which she has no permission. She has married into enormous wealth and seems perfectly content with the outcome.

Family life

Most affluent medieval urban households were social hubs: servants bustled about their work inside and outside the home, cleaning, cooking, receiving visitors, taking and bringing back messages, running errands. Visitors and guests would need to be welcomed and sometimes accommodated. Tradespeople may have been working on the property or offering goods and services. Most houses had some form of stabling arrangements for the horses essential for transport and some kept their own livestock. Sons and daughters would have their own allotted tasks and responsibilities. This malleable domestic unit which continued into early modern societies was based on the Roman *domus*, a domicile controlled by the 'paterfamilias', the father of the family, who under the law had *patria potestas*, fatherly power which placed everything under his control. The word 'patriarchy' is descended from these historical blueprints.

Within his household the paterfamilias/patriarch was supreme governor with power to sell, barter, and impose sanctions and discipline. In Roman times this power could even include the right to decide if a transgression such as adultery were to be punished by death. However, the law as codified by Emperor Justinian I was couched in so many ifs, buts and special circumstances it seems that the legislation acted more as a deliberate deterrent than an encouragement to kill. For example, under the Justinian Code a paterfamilias would be excused the killing of his adulterous wife and her lover only if three conditions were simultaneous or immediately consecutive: if the sexual act were committed in the family home; if the adulterers were caught in the act; and if death was immediate, that is brought about by uncontrollable, momentary passion.

The Code amusingly (?) states that if the adulterous act were committed in a 'summerhouse' or some other place, i.e. not the main family residence, the paterfamilias had no legal right to perpetrate violence on either of the

Context

The Justinian Code, the *Corpus Juris Civilis* ('Body of Civil Law'), is a four-part Latin encyclopaedia of Roman law issued from 529 to 534 by order of Justinian I. The Code became the sole source of law; reference to any other legal source, including the original texts from which the Code had been compiled, was forbidden. In the Middle Ages it became the foundation of all civil law across Europe and thus can be described as the mainspring of the Western legal tradition.

participants. Adultery gave a husband the right to divorce his wife but if a man accused his wife of adultery and could not prove it, she could divorce him. Roman law as exemplified in the Code was quite equitable when it came to divorce: men had five legal reasons and women had six. Male adultery was taken very seriously. Here is a flavour: 'The wife of a man convicted of adultery is entitled to possession of her dowry and the prenuptial donation'. If a woman committed adultery and her husband divorced her she would receive two-thirds of any property she brought with her into the marriage unless she had children when the husband was legally required to keep the property intact to give to the children when they came of age.

The Justinian Code made excess violence against women a very serious crime; the paterfamilias would have to pay directly to the woman an amount identical to the prenuptial dowry if any beating meted out was too extreme: 'if a man should beat his wife with a whip or rod without legitimate cause the marriage will not be dissolved but she will get a sum of money from his other property equal to the prenuptial donation'. In other words the husband would liable to pay a hefty fine for his cruelty. These Roman notions continued into medieval and Tudor times, though with the rise and eventual cultural domination of Christianity, the more liberal Roman ideas about divorce were reined in. Where beating did take place in sixteenth- and seventeenth-century England, it could be administered with a whip or a rod as both items had been mentioned by name in the Justinian Code; if a husband did physically chastise without good legal reason then the violence was seen to be unjustified and the woman's family could seek redress through the legal system. The church frequently spoke out against the undesirability of violence against women, though less so against children, who had less protection under the law.

A 1588 woodcut of domestic assault ▶
from a German deck of playing cards
('Kartenspielbuch' of Jost Amman).
Here, the violence is not condoned but is
depicted as being the 'beastly' behaviour
of a 'choleric' man

For modern people notions of appropriate levels of violence are disturbing and outlandish: how much violence is or was extreme or excessive? Why was the primary punishment for extreme domestic violence linked to money and a wife's 'worth' in financial terms based on dowry arrangements which were themselves an equation of a woman's value in a commercial context? The patriarch also had responsibilities of protection and guardianship so domestic arrangements were contractual: in essence there were penalty clauses which stipulated punishments if the terms of the contract were not observed. The wife's family could become very awkward if it were believed that she was suffering in some way. Late medieval and early modern family life was complicated and very different to our understanding of it now. Life for women was not always one spent under the yoke of male control, though it seems fair to say that the poorer the woman, the less likely she would be to have much realistic opportunity of resorting to the law. As ever, life for the wealthy was always easier.

Under certain circumstances men, particularly those from the merchant class who by necessity had to spend considerable periods of time away from home, would cede patriarchal power to their wives so that the family business could run from the *domus* undisturbed.

◀ 'The Arnolfini Wedding', a 1484 painting by Dutch painter Jan van Eyck

Marriage and gender roles

The painting shown on p.35 is variously known as 'The Arnolfini Wedding', 'The Arnolfini Betrothal' or 'The Arnolfini Portrait'. Art experts cannot agree on what the painting depicts, beyond some form of oath-taking symbolised by the discarded footwear and the single lit candle. However, the placement of the two figures can seem to suggest conventional fifteenth-century views of marriage and gender roles – the woman (sometimes identified as Giovanna Cenami) stands near the bed and is central within the room, symbolic of her role as the 'heart' of the house, whereas the man (identified as Giovanni Arnolfini) stands near the open window, symbolic of his role in the outside world. His large hat symbolises his wealth but also the power of his role as 'head' of the household. Arnolfini looks directly at the viewer, his wife gazes in the direction of her husband. His right hand is vertically raised, representing his commanding position of authority, while she has her right hand in a lower, horizontal, and perhaps more submissive pose. Is her gaze submissive or confident? She is clearly not looking down at the floor as brow-beaten or dominated women would, so the painting intrigues. Is she pregnant? The symbolism behind the action of the couple's joined hands is also the topic of much debate: is what is being painted a marriage contract or something else? Erwin Panofsky (1910–1968) interprets the gesture as a 'marital oath' but the man is grasping the woman's right hand with his *left* hand, which leads Margaret D. Carroll in *Painting and Politics in Northern Europe* (Penn State University Press, 2008) to suggest that the painting deploys the imagery of a contract between an *already* married couple, giving the wife the authority to act on her husband's behalf in business dealings. Carroll identifies Arnolfini's raised right hand as a gesture of oath-taking known as '*fidem levare*' (i.e. to raise, intensify or amplify a pre-existing pledge of faith), and his joining hands with his wife (man left; woman right) as a gesture of consent known as '*fides manualis*', a pledge of faith symbolically transferred from the hand.

▲ A detail from the Arnolphini wedding by Jan van Eyck

That her right hand is lying over his left hand is symbolic of her power and – presumably temporary – dominion. So to Carroll, the painting symbolises a pre-existing marriage where the woman is trusted as an equal and has been given complete power of attorney or, in the words of the play, has been given 'all'. So are women oppressed slaves or trusted and loved partners? Medieval and early modern marriage arrangements and customs are complex and defy simplistic modern attempts to explain or categorise them.

For modern people it may be impossible to know precisely how people behaved under such marital arrangements. We have been socialised and educated differently. We think different thoughts. However, it is necessary that we try to understand how people functioned so we can better understand Shakespeare's craft. Baptista is an urban sophisticate who 'plays a merchant's part' and clearly knows how to drive a hard bargain but at least he makes arrangements for Katherine to be married before Bianca. His reasons cannot all be selfish or mercenary because as a father he would have to pay out a dowry to a daughter's prospective husband, which is what he does to Petruchio *twice* in the play: the first time in Act 2, Scene 1, when he agrees to give Petruchio 'After my death, the one half of my lands, / And in possession twenty thousand crowns'; the second dowry is a spontaneous gift of 'twenty thousand crowns, Another dowry' (Act 5, Scene 2) awarded to Petruchio for the change he has apparently wrought in Katherine. Baptista does not seek to sell Katherine off to the highest bidder and in Act 2 even tells Petruchio that he must obtain Katherine's love for that is 'all in all'. Baptista himself will not benefit materially from Bianca's marriage though there will perhaps be more social cachet for him to be linked to Vincentio and Lucentio, once of Florence but now of Pisa, than suburban Paduan neighbours like Hortensio and Gremio.

Katherine demonstrates that she resents being given orders and told what to do: 'What, shall I be appointed hours, as though, belike, / I knew not what to take and what to leave?' (Act 1, Scene 1); 'Do what though canst, I will not go today, / No, nor tomorrow – not till I please myself' (Act 3, Scene 2) and claims equality on several occasions, finding favour with modern audiences who view notions of female inequality distasteful.

Build critical skills

Is Katherine's bad behaviour in the early part of the play justified? Use the examples offered here and identify more of your own to support your view.

CRITICAL VIEW

Marilyn French, *Shakespeare's Division of Experience* (New York, Ballantine, 1981), argues that Katherine's shrewishness is a 'disguise … forced on her by a neglectful father, a sly sister, and an unsympathetic society'. This view acknowledges Katherine's bad behaviour but justifies it by placing it against traumatising and cruel social and familial contexts centred on the concept of households run and organised by patriarchs.

When Aristotle argued that the most fundamental form of independent political association was the heterosexual union in a household which formed one unit of government and labour, he was making a very serious point. Yes, the household was the starting point for an ascending hierarchy of political associations going right up to government level and, yes again, Tudor households were arranged in hierarchies. However, much humour in comedy frequently subverts ideas of social order, perhaps nowhere more incessantly and incisively as in *The Taming of the Shrew*. The servants, particularly Tranio, subvert the usual power patterns which existed between masters and servants in Tudor England. One interpretation of this frequently reinterpreted play is that Katherine subverts the existing social order in Padua; then Petruchio – comically subversive to his very roots of behaviour and dress – subverts Katherine because her violence demeans her and disguises her true inner beauty; and finally Petruchio and Katherine as a couple – she liberated, he the rebel who set her on her own path to freedom – subvert the two sham, empty and dishonest marriages of Lucentio to Bianca and Hortensio to the widow.

This final subversion not only disrupts Paduan society but makes the English audience question its own attitudes to power structures in English marriage and family life. We laugh; we think; we apply what we think to our lives and 'aright ourselves': that is the particular gift of comedy.

Taking it further ▶

Maurice Hunt, 'Homeopathy in Shakespearean Comedy and Romance' (1988) argues that Petruchio helps his 'patient to achieve a truer self, one freed from … the trap of shrewishness'. Even if you think Katherine was trapped at the beginning of the play but is liberated at the conclusion, you will need to work out how much of her progress is down to her own efforts. Also, is 'patient' an accurate term to use for Katherine?

Human nature and animal behaviour

The word 'shrew' and its derivatives are applied to Katherine on 15 occasions in the play. The Induction has already prepared the audience for the frequent utilisation of animal imagery when human behaviour falls short of the expectations of those who hold power. The lord out hunting with 'hounds' compares Sly to a 'monstrous beast' and 'a swine'. Part of the jest is to convince Sly that he has a stable of fine horses and a kennel of hounds but when he awakes he initially seems to know that he is 'by transmutation a bear-herd' before his doubts begin.

Build critical skills

'Transmutation' is a fascinating word for Shakespeare to select here. It means the process or act of changing from one thing to another. Sly is aware that he is in a continuous state of flux, now a tinker, once a bear-herd (a keeper of tame performing bears), by birth a pedlar, but educated to be a card-maker (maker of wool-combs). Why not now a lord? To what extent do you agree that Katherine is in a perpetual state of transmutation in the play?

He is told he can have 'twenty caged nightingales' sing for him or he can go out hawking on horseback or let his greyhounds course stags. When Petruchio reveals his plans for dealing with his 'shrew' in Act 2, Scene 1 he says nothing about hunting or falconry but brings in a reference from the Induction: 'Say that she rail, why then I'll tell her plain / She sings as sweetly as the nightingale' to force Katherine to see herself as a fictive, made-up 'Kate' instead of her true self; in other words just as the lord did with Sly to make the appearance more real than the fact. 'Shrew imagery dominates the first half of the play but falconry and hawking imagery dominates the second half' (Brian Morris, Arden Shakespeare, *The Taming of the Shrew*, 1981 edition). Can Petruchio's intervention be said to be giving Katherine wings?

CRITICAL VIEW

Caroline Spurgeon (*Shakespeare's Imagery and What it Tells Us*, 1935) writes: 'Shakespeare's images from birds form by far the largest section drawn from any single class of objects' (apart from humans), citing 'the soaring of ... the hawk, the "fell swoop" of the kite ... the confident flight of the falcon, "towering in her pride of place"'. Shakespeare invariably refers to hawks as 'she', because it is the female, or peregrine falcon, that is used for hunting, since the female is bigger, stronger and faster than the male.

Gerald Lascelles in *Shakespeare's England* (OUP, 1916) claims that the technical terms of falconry were so well known in all households rich and poor that Petruchio's techniques would have needed no explanation.

Petruchio is attempting to 'man' her, watching her, keeping her awake and limiting food so that the bird settles. However, modern audiences frequently misunderstand Petruchio's actions because our understanding of falconry has evaporated.

In traditional hawking, as outlined by Symon Latham in *The Falcon's Lure and Cure* (see illustration), once tameness was achieved, testing the bird for obedience was necessary to see how successful the training had been.

Lascelles recounts: 'In a few weeks our hawk will display no fear of men or dogs even when bareheaded in the open air … When this stage has been reached there is no more in the way of training to be done but to accustom the hawk to fly to the lure … At first she is for safety's sake confined by a creance or long light line, but ere long she is flown loose altogether and … is ready to be entered to the quarry which she is destined to pursue.' Via a series of vignettes Shakespeare shows the audience how Petruchio tests Katherine at distances increasingly further and further away from home in a similar way to how a falconer gives his bird more and more latitude until she knows 'her keeper's call'. The argument about the right time of day in Act 4, Scene 3 is revisited and reworked in Act 4, Scene 5 when it becomes the famous dispute about the sun and the moon with Petruchio's contentious and clearly erroneous comment about the brightness of the moon. It would appear that Katherine has not quite learned her lesson, however, and Petruchio threatens to go back to square one in the form of returning home and beginning the process all over again. Hortensio prompts her: 'Say as he says, or we shall never go' and Katherine, perhaps desirous of a simple life, complies and the journey is resumed. Petruchio doggedly makes her say that she sees the world is as he sees it: 'I say it is the moon,' he insists and she concurs.

The second test occurs immediately afterwards when the couple meet Vincentio. Petruchio raises the stakes here as the test involves a third person, a stranger, and if it fails Katherine will perhaps be exposed to public ridicule, the thing she fears the most. By now, however, Katherine knows the rules of Petruchio's game and gleefully, so it would seem, joins in. A further test occurs in Act 5, Scene 1 when, following Petruchio's and Katherine's eavesdropping on the unfolding disguise plot, he asks her for a public kiss. When she shyly demurs he threatens to go home yet again but as she grants him the kiss she says 'Now pray thee love, stay.' Her language now utilises 'thee' not the more formal 'you' of early Act 4 and the line is said with what appears to be genuine affection.

The final scene represents Katherine's greatest test but because of the kiss we have recently witnessed the audience is not sure whether it is a straightforward test of obedience, as was the argument about the time, or whether it has become a test of love and loyalty. The final test is certainly the most public and in an echo of the hawking manuals Katherine is required to 'betray no fear' and do so 'bareheaded': 'Katherine, that cap of yours becomes you not: / Off with that bauble — throw it underfoot.' At this point the stage directions simply read 'She obeys'. That she goes on to give her sermon about wifely duty comes as

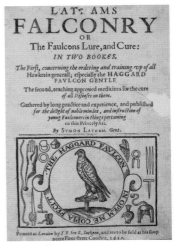

▲ Symon Latham's *The Falcon's Lure and Cure*

Context

In the *Book of Saint Albans* (1486) Benedictine prioress Juliana Berners lists raptors with their appropriate social rank: i.e. an eagle for an Emperor; a gyrfalcon for a King; a peregrine for an Earl; a merlin for a Lady; a sparrow-hawk for a Priest; a kestrel for a Knave. How much notice Tudor falconers took of the social categories in the book is debatable.

a surprise to the other characters but not, perhaps, to the audience, who have been pointed in this direction by Shakespeare's subtle layering of the tests, each containing a greater degree of difficulty than the one before.

Build critical skills

Nichola McAuliffe, who has played Katherine twice, believes that when Petruchio denies Katherine sleep and food, he is describing how human and animal endure the same deprivations: 'If you know anything about falconry, you would know that you have to go through this with the bird: if it's cruel, it's cruel to yourself, too.' How far do you think that Petruchio's behaviour to Katherine is different to the lord's behaviour to Sly in the Induction?

▲ A medieval image showing a happy couple out with a falcon.

The battle of the sexes

Petruchio mentions Xanthippe, Socrates' shrewish wife who is represented in classical and medieval literature in comic terms: one story is that after haranguing Socrates, who refused to get annoyed, she emptied a chamber pot over his head at which point her philosophical husband placidly remarked, 'Ah, yes. After the thunder comes the rain.' Xanthippe tore off Socrates' coat in the Athenian marketplace and his friends goaded him to chastise her physically but he refused on the grounds that a couple's private disagreements were not to be made a spectator sport. Shakespeare gives a flavour of Socratic wisdom to Petruchio: when Katherine is being difficult in a public place by demanding they go into the wedding feast in Act 3, Scene 2, Petruchio whisks her away to his own home where he can curb her 'headstrong humour' in relative privacy. Petruchio does not want to destroy Katherine's spirit; he wants to turn it to a better purpose.

Build critical skills

What thematic links can you make between *The Taming of the Shrew* and any other literature texts, particularly dramatic texts that you have studied?

CRITICAL VIEW

Tita French Baumlin in 'Petruchio the Sophist and Language as Creation in *The Taming of the Shrew*', *Studies in English Literature* 29 (1989) praises Petruchio as a 'sophistic rhetorician' who transforms 'an isolated, selfish, dysfunctional personality into a socially integrated woman at peace with herself and the world'. Baumlin argues that Petruchio's skill in argument, debate and his all-round way with words convinces Katherine of his rightness.

In *The Republic* Plato writes of Socrates' belief that in his imagined 'best city' women of 'spirit and intelligence' should be educated along with their male equals to enable them to become rulers. Education must precede authority: Petruchio embellishes the point when he tells Katherine in Act 4, Scene 3 that when she is 'gentle' she can have rewards. He could be said to be following the Socratic method.

English precedents of shrewish women arrive via the mystery and morality plays of the High Medieval Era.

Context

Mystery plays (from the Latin *misterium* meaning 'occupation') are among the earliest dramatic forms in medieval Europe; they reworked Bible stories. In the York play *The Flood*, Noah's wife wants to go back to collect her belongings, insisting her friends and relations must come too; in the Chester play she wants to stay drinking with her 'gossips'; in Towneley she wants to finish her 'spinning' and seems unable to look beyond her current profitable occupation.

cycle — a group of texts sharing a common subject or theme.

In the York Fishers' and Mariners' play *The Flood*, Mrs Noah refuses to join her family on the Ark when her husband asks: 'Telle him I will come no narre'. In *Shrew* this is echoed in the widow's refusal to come to Hortensio's request in Act 5, Scene 2: 'She will not come.' In the Chester and Wakefield (Towneley) **cycles** she assaults her husband as he tries to save her when she is carried on board. However, once on the Ark (a metaphor for Mother Church), she changes and learns to be compliant and useful. In the Wakefield version (*Processus Noe*) she is transformed from a rebellious and violent troublemaker into a willing and helpful joint-captain of the Ark to whom Noah defers when seeking advice about which bird to send off first in search of land. Can it be coincidence that Shakespeare gives Petruchio so many maritime references in his language? The playwright clearly wants to portray marriage as an Ark 'new-built' on Katherine's virtue (Act 5, Scene 2) representing 'peace, love and quiet life' after the storms of violence and stubbornness have raised troubled waters.

A medieval image of ▶ Noah's Ark where Noah and his wife, now reconciled after her violent outburst, have joint command of the vessel and save humankind and all the animals

Target your thinking

● How can a thorough understanding of the play's characterisation extend your knowledge of the text? It is useful to remember that Shakespeare uses his characters to present themes to the audience. (**AO1** and **AO2**)

Induction

Sly

We first see Sly as a drunken rustic lout in his own environment but by Induction, Scene 2 he is dressed in fine robes and is in a luxurious apartment, a 'drinks-like-a-fish out of water' if you will. Sly's sense of self is disrupted by the lord's trick and, though his language alters to become more like the lord's, he is still in some sense essentially himself – the earthy, believable and far from perfect tinker: he still wants 'small ale' and wants his 'wife' to 'undress' and 'come to bed'. He is interested in sex not romance but his perceptions alter along with the ways he describes the world.

In many ways Sly's life on stage mirrors Katherine's: they are both transformed; he certainly against his will as no consent can be granted when drunk and incapable. Katherine's consent is debatable but she is silent for the 26 lines of Act 2, Scene 1 before her exit in line 328 so some form of consent may be assumed. By the conclusion of the play Katherine may be happy but we do not see the conclusion of Sly's transformation. The actor playing Sly almost invariably doubles up as Petruchio, which can give a dream-like quality to the play proper and make the whole experience a kind of fantasy which has a definite beginning but no definite end. Sly is still out there somewhere in the theatre of the mind watching a play he wishes 'were done'.

The lord

Is the lord an agent of some form of social justice cleaning up the streets for the good of wider society or is he a spiteful Puritanical moralist whose sense of entitlement is so extensive that he feels he is within his rights to alter people's lives for his own 'sport'? Certainly his hunting dogs have affected names such as Clowder, Merriman and Echo and, like many modern toffs, the lord and his entourage get very excited, loudly quacking and braying about which dog is the best. On this evidence he does not appear to be an intellectual giant. His plan to 'practise' on Sly seems to have no serious moral undercurrent and he terms it a 'jest'. That we do not see the outcome of the lord's jest adds to the enigma.

Bartholomew

The actor playing Bartholomew usually doubles up as Biondello or Grumio. His importance lies in the fact that he is nominated to play the part of Sly's wife in the Induction's subterfuge and thus Bartholomew's allegorical and symbolic importance is huge. The sexual comedy between Bartholomew and Sly is funny but makes a serious point about a wife's roles and responsibilities. He claims 'I am your wife in all obedience' and so hints at a model of wifely perfection but Bartholomew still skilfully manages to avoid having sex with Sly, thus demonstrating that even an 'obedient wife' has control over her own decisions. This may be a Shakespearean hint that even women who say they are obedient to their husbands will find ways of asserting themselves in important matters. Bartholomew, like Sly, does not have a theatrical ending: the page pretending to be a dutiful wife is out there somewhere surveying an empty stage.

Main play

Katherine

CRITICAL VIEW

George Bernard Shaw condemns Petruchio for his 'domineering cruelty' (spoof letter to the *Pall Mall Gazette*, 1889). Mark Van Doren argues that we must 'confess' that Petruchio is 'torturing' Katherine during his 'taming' of her (1939). These readings see the arc of the play as diminishing Katherine, reducing or even erasing her entirely; other critics see in the play an arc of growth and development for Katherine.

Who is Katherina Minola? What sort of identity does she have? The name Kate is shorter and more familiar to modern students than Katherina but a 'cate' is also a dainty morsel; when Petruchio first calls her Kate it can be seen as an attempt to belittle and patronise her and the shortened version of her name links to the 'household-stuff' to which Petruchio compares her later. However, he has just heard Baptista refer to her as 'my daughter Kate' and Bianca calls her 'sister Kate' so he could be following family precedent. However, Baptista calls her Katherina *and* Katherine, as do Gremio and Hortensio. The response she gives Petruchio on first meeting stands as testimony that she will not be belittled: 'They call me Katherine that do talk of me.' She refers to herself by name four times in the play and uses Katherine *each time*. Therefore in her own head she is only ever Katherine and that is why we use that version of her name in this book.

Is she even a 'shrew' at all? She is certainly aware of her own desires and says she will 'please herself' twice in Act 2, so is clearly aware of herself and of what she thinks she wants, but the male Paduans seem to exaggerate her shrewishness. It can be argued that she is first defined and then redefined by the power of the male tongue rather than by the power of her own tongue and to this purpose Shakespeare gives her less than half of the number of lines he attributes to Petruchio. She is undoubtedly initially violent and out of control, threatening violence often and resorting to it on six separate occasions in the play, with its zenith occurring in Act 2, Scene 1. Such violence is evidence of her essential early unhappiness and frustration. She is older – perhaps considerably older – than Bianca, is openly hostile to potential suitors Hortensio and Gremio, and is more intelligent and spirited than both. Petruchio clearly changes her but is it for good or ill? There is a brand of criticism which sees the changes as forced, unnatural, cruel or unnecessary.

By Act 5 she is still forceful but is now eloquent and measured, as her language indicates. She insists that marriage can bring erotic and emotional liberation if men but especially women accept their natural boundaries. Some feminists are outraged by this philosophy, arguing that Katherine has betrayed or has been forced to betray her gender by becoming a male sexual fantasy. Opponents of this view contend that Katherine is now content and happy whereas she was miserable and unfulfilled before. Most historicist analyses see in Katherine's later self an improvement on her earlier self, pointing out that Elizabethan society did not prioritise keeping single women in a state of happiness outside of marriage. Self-improvement, personal and spiritual was a duty for cultured Elizabethans.

Self-improvement, personal and spiritual was a duty for cultured Elizabethans

Historicists do not find it outrageous that Katherine ends the play conforming to the usual notions of a happy marriage for the era. What lasting happiness could Katherine achieve in Baptista's *domus* when she has been unhappy there from the outset? How can Katherine be happy in an environment which has already made her so miserable as to reduce to nothing her good qualities and amplify her defects? Petruchio wants Katherine to become 'conformable' because her violence has made her — as she herself acknowledges — 'muddy, ill-seeming, thick, bereft of beauty' but Petruchio has noticed and has been inspired by her 'beauty', inner and exterior. The changes will benefit both of them and their marriage will be sexual, joyous and entirely compatible.

Bianca

On first glance, Bianca (meaning 'white' in Italian) may seem to represent silent female Elizabethan conformity, obeying her father and attracting a string of suitors. However, as the principal female in the sub-plot she represents the woman who only pretends to conform to get her own way, whereas in the main plot Katherine's behaviour is an honest reflection of how she feels. Bianca, like Katherine, makes it clear that she will 'please herself' but only says so in the company of her suitors who are besotted with her and who will not question her authority. Here is a woman who clearly knows the differences between public and private behaviour and as the play progresses she speaks more assertively to Lucentio. At the play's conclusion she has swapped roles with her sister: it is Bianca not Katherine who is the real shrew and her domination of her husband seems set to continue.

Baptista

Many critics argue that Baptista is a bad or even a dysfunctional father who treats Katherine unfairly. Rebecca Warren (York Notes, 2005 edition) claims he is 'a conventional Elizabethan patriarch. He is attached to at least one of his daughters (Bianca), but views both as objects to be bartered on the marriage market.' Such a critique can lure actors into offering one-dimensional presentations of Baptista but, as the Commentary sections of this guide indicate, it could be argued that he is not such a bad father: Baptista only agrees to

CRITICAL VIEW

'Bianca gives women a very bad name', argues Michelle Gomez, who played Katherine for the Royal Shakespeare Company in 2008. 'She is the manipulative, backstabbing, awful version of what women are, fluttering her eyelids to get what she wants.'

Tranio/Lucentio's offer of marriage in Act 2, Scene 1 when he learns that Bianca will be assured of fabulous wealth if she is left a widow. He will not personally gain materially or financially from this arrangement. Warren also claims that Baptista 'disregards his eldest daughter's feelings … he wants to be rid of' Katherine, but Baptista insists in Act 2, Scene 1 that Petruchio must obtain Katherine's love, though he makes no such demands of Bianca's suitors.

Good actors often show that Baptista has reserves of affection for his troubled elder child and that Katherine misunderstands his motives as much if not more than he misunderstands hers. His demand that Katherine needs to be married before he will contemplate a match for Bianca has been called 'selfish', 'canny' and 'mercenary' but the alternative – to allow Bianca to marry first – would be to relegate Katherine even further down the pecking order and perhaps to condemn her to a life of solitude without the benefits that Elizabethan marriage could bring a woman. The dowry he offers Petruchio is staggeringly high and will ensure that, financially at least, Katherine is set up for life. In offering a second dowry for her transformation in Act 5 he ensures that Katherine's 'third', should she be widowed, is double what it was before her change. If Baptista were completely mercenary and wanted rid of her it is unlikely that he would have placed more money than was necessary into her new family. In rewarding Petruchio he is rewarding Katherine too. Though Baptista's motives and behaviour may be difficult for modern audiences to understand, he is not a cruel or unthinking father for his era.

Lucentio

In one sense Lucentio is constructed as a cosmopolitan sophisticate, having been born in Pisa and brought up in Florence. Despite his travels, Lucentio seems to have an imprecise knowledge of geography: when he arrives to study in Padua he claims it is in Lombardy. Ortelius' map of Europe, perhaps known to Shakespeare, made the same mistake so Lucentio may be echoing his creator's faulty knowledge. Another view is that Shakespeare did know about Italian geography but by making Lucentio ignorant the playwright begins to construct an unreliable quality about him. Lucentio's early notion that he wishes to 'plunge' himself into the 'deep waters' of knowledge are typical of other Shakespearean rich young men who will be side-tracked by love.

Lucentio, the attractive outsider, falls in love with Bianca at first sight without even hearing her speak. He is in many ways a typical male principal lover of sixteenth-century drama: wealthy, charming and conventional. The actor playing him has to be stereotypically handsome enough to convince the audience that his veneer will succeed with the equally stereotypical Bianca. However, he is at heart a liar, prepared to hoodwink Baptista via his disguise as Licio. In many ways he is overshadowed by his servant Tranio who has a much fuller role in the play and, as the play progresses, Lucentio seems to not just rely on his servants but to need them to run his schemes. In the best productions his early raffish charm is replaced by a rather empty docility which can be presented as a sort of

Context

Young men giving up love for study features in Shakespeare's *Love's Labour's Lost* (written close to *Shrew*) when Ferdinand, Longaville, Dumain and the more realistic Berowne swear to have no contact with women during their Academy course. Their good intentions are overtaken by more earthly passions and the men learn an important lesson: nature meant them to be lovers, not academics.

complacent upper-class stupidity. Against the manly Petruchio he is made to look puny and inadequate in the final scene when the audience can see that he is well matched with his shallow new wife.

Tranio

Tranio is the resourceful, clever servant typical of Elizabethan and Jacobean theatre whose contributions to the disguise plan enable Lucentio to win Bianca. He is knowledgeable in Latin and has the self-assurance and confidence to pass as Lucentio in Padua. His name first features in Roman playwright Plautus' (254–184 BC) *Mostellaria* ('*The Haunted House*') in which Tranio, a slave owned by Theopropides, acts swiftly to help Theopropides' son Philolaches out of a pickle concerning Philematium, a 'music girl' courtesan he has freed from slavery via a loan. The plot revolves around Tranio, a sophisticated city-dweller, trying to convince the returning Theopropides that his house is locked up because it is haunted when in reality Philolaches, Philematium and their friends are hiding within, having been living a life of constant pleasure for the last three years. Plautus' Tranio is as capable in Greek as Shakespeare's is in Latin and both are cleverer than their masters. Intriguingly Grumio, in the guise of 'a country slave' also owned by Theopropides, appears as a character in *Mostellaria* so it is likely that Shakespeare was very familiar with this and other Plautine plays.

> ## Context
>
> ### Shakespeare's use of *Mostellaria*
>
> A Tranio and a Grumio appear in both. Comedy ensues from the young male lover observing a female on the street. Comic knocking on doors and quibbles about money, a woman being 'bought' by a man so he can marry her occur in both plays. Both Tranios are threatened with a beating and run away but both are forgiven at the end.

It is important that Tranio, whose name is a Latin derivative of the Greek word for 'revealer', acts as a persuader to Lucentio in his quest for Bianca, telling his master, in among the references to Aristotle, Ovid and **Lily's Latin grammar**, that 'no profit grows where is no pleasure ta'en', thus revealing the folly of living a life at variance with Lucentio's true nature.

Biondello

Biondello transmutes from being a gullible servant at the beginning of the play, when he believes that Lucentio is a fugitive murderer, into a resourceful 'cheeky-chappie' banterer who gives a brilliantly comic description of Petruchio's wedding attire and who hustles Lucentio and Bianca off stage in Act 5, Scene 1, seeming to acquire some of Tranio's lustre and verbal flair as the play progresses.

William Lily or Lilly (1468–1523) was the author of *Grammar of Latin in English: An Introduction of the Eyght Partes of Speche, and the Construction of the Same*. In 1542 Henry VIII authorised it as the sole Latin grammar textbook to be used in schools. It was used for more than 300 years. Shakespeare refers to it several times in his plays, notably Act 2, Scene 1 of Henry IV, Part 1: "Homo is a common name to all men".

Hortensio

Initially presented as Petruchio's old friend, Hortensio performs the important plot function of introducing Petruchio to the idea of Katherine. Unlike his virile friend, Hortensio has no success with women and his failures drive much of the comedy: Bianca rejects him, Katherine batters him with the lute and his widow ignores him. His weakness is the opposite of Petruchio's muscular vigour and his efforts to emulate his friend's powerful techniques and behaviour are misplaced. He is to all intents and purposes impotent and is included in the play as an illustration that even in a patriarchy some men, even wealthy ones, hold no real power at all.

Gremio

Gremio is the stock old man from classical and Italian drama with an inappropriate interest in a young woman. In many ways he represents the worst side of manhood: he complains about and is threatened by Katherine's scolding and his insults that she is a 'fiend of hell' and a 'devil' are exaggerations which show the extent of Katherine's social isolation. After he loses the auction he is of little importance to the plot but he does lurk around commenting on various twists in the action. Once he has lost Bianca, he states that he will console himself with the prospect of a good meal, thus indicating that Shakespeare presents him not only as a low-ambition contrast to the completely successful and dynamic Petruchio but also as a more down-to-earth contrast to the successful wooer but failed romantic and unsuccessful husband Lucentio.

Petruchio

To play Petruchio is to have an unrivalled opportunity for entertaining an audience; his behaviour can be farcical and his first appearance puts him at the heart of some of the slapstick. However, he is psychologically energetic and linguistically adept and skilful, his speeches showing a great descriptive verve. His early declamations in Act 1 are muscular, utilising the dynamic language of battles and adventure; by the middle of the play his language is witty and sexually suggestive; and by Act 4 his speeches have taken on a more philosophical tone.

How an audience responds to Petruchio depends on how the director presents him and whether the production shows him as humane, comic, malevolently misogynistic, a proto-feminist, an adventurer or a psychopath. The audience must try to understand him in relation to how Katherine is presented: is she essentially afraid and misunderstood and is her violence a manifestation of her unhappiness or is she 'stark mad', needing a cure?

What is not in doubt is Petruchio's economic, social and geographical mobility compared to hers. He is the captain of his own fate, travelling widely throughout Italy, making his own decisions. If we take him at face value he is a fortune-hunter on the prowl for a wealthy wife and does not care if she be 'foul', 'old',

Context

Gremio is a 'pantaloon' (Italian 'pantalone'), a stock character from the Italian *Commedia dell'arte* tradition, a comic old man with a sexual and marital interest in younger women. He gets his name from his stock-in-trade comedy trousers known as pantaloons. I have seen him in a modern production hilariously portrayed as an elderly professional golfer. Priceless.

'curst', 'shrewd' or 'rough' so long as 'money comes' with her. Yet to take Petruchio at face value is a dangerous business because his 'faces' alter as the play develops. Is he entirely serious in Act 1, Scene 1 or is he acting a part for the more conservative Paduans? We must not lose sight of genre: the purpose of comedy is first to create laughter and then to make the audience think. What if he is mercenary before he sees Katherine but smitten with her beautiful potential when they meet? That he is mercenary at all can be thrown into very serious doubt by his 'assurance' given to Baptista in Act 2, Scene 1 that in the event of her widowhood Katherine will have 'all' his 'lands and leases', an extraordinarily generous settlement far exceeding the legal third he was obliged to leave her. Is this the act of a mercenary and cold-blooded proto venture capitalist? The script allows many permutations of Petruchio's behaviour and motives. He claims he will 'board' Katherine (such nautical terms are common to Petruchio in the first two acts) and he grapples his way into her life like a pirate boarding a rival vessel.

In the custody of a talented actor Petruchio overwhelms the audience as much as he seems to dumbfound and wrong-foot Katherine. To many observers it may appear that the taming in earnest begins in Act 4 but Petruchio's behaviour has always been at odds with the expectations of those around him and he behaves unexpectedly at every turn, leading onlookers to comment that he – as well as Katherine – is 'mad'. Consequently the wedding ceremony and its raucous aftermath may look unhinged and incongruous but, like **Drake's raid on Cadiz**, everything has been methodically planned and prepared beforehand. Is it peculiar that Petruchio's ambitions, despite his swashbuckling persona, are actually quite modest and conform to the religious ideals of the times? He declares that he values domestic peace and harmony above all else. The clamorous din he kicks up is intended to secure a quiet life at home. Petruchio certainly does not resort to physical violence despite the provocation of the slap when he and Katherine first meet; though to deprive her of food, sleep and sex on her wedding night can be seen as cruel and unusual behaviour. He is certainly and self-consciously eccentric and the audience is encouraged by Shakespeare to recognise that Petruchio is acting a part, playing his role as a 'mad brained rudesby full of spleen' to educate and reform his wife. By the end of the play it is clear that he is more than satisfied with Katherine and his declaration, 'Why, there's a wench! Come on, and kiss me, Kate' indicates approval as well as genuine loving affection and sexual attraction.

Grumio

This character's name can be traced back to the Greek word for dirt or rubbish and the joke is that he is dirty in appearance and clothing. In *Mostellaria* Tranio insults him with a tirade of dirt- and stench-related jokes: 'you stink of garlic, you unmistakable piece of filth, you clod, you he-goat, you pig-sty, you mixture of dog and she-goat …' Grumio is akin to the licensed fool of the royal courts allowed to backchat his social superiors and join in the comic banter as long as his essential motives are loyal and he supports his master.

Build critical skills

Read through Petruchio's speeches choosing examples of his adventurous imagery in Act 1, his witty and suggestive speech in Act 3 and his philosophical tone in Act 4. How does your collection of lines help to chart the development of his character?

In April 1587 an English naval force commanded by Francis Drake attacked the Spanish fleet in Cadiz and thereafter raided parts of Spain and Portugal, destroying more than 100 vessels, at the cost of some 300,000 crowns to the Spanish authorities. The planned invasion of England was delayed by one year: Drake referred to the action as 'singeing the King of Spain's beard'. The raid proved the superiority of English seamanship over the Spanish and was a significant morale-booster.

Grumio is Petruchio's foil, taking part in his anarchic schemes with relish; in this sense he is every bit as helpful to Petruchio as Tranio is to Lucentio though, unlike Tranio, Grumio is not notably more intelligent than his master. In modern terms he is a sidekick, a swashbuckling hero's assistant, though it is interesting to note that Biondello refers to him as a 'lackey', a word carrying the Elizabethan meaning of footman who 'lacked eyes', i.e. who could keep his master's secrets and chose not to see any shortcomings. In modern usage, especially in comics, a lackey can be a henchman, i.e. a villain's assistant. Critics who dislike Petruchio pounce on this meaning, seeing in Grumio not a comic footman but a partner in crime, making the duo more Burke and Hare than Reeves and Mortimer. The character Baldrick in the *Blackadder* TV comedies is based on the notion of the unkempt, filthy servant drawn into his master's schemes but sometimes coming up with an often stupid 'cunning plan' of his own. Pearce Quigley in Toby Frow's 2012 Globe production even used some of Tony Robinson's, the original Baldrick's, vocal patterns and intonations. The audience loved it.

Pedant

It would be easy to see the pedant as a stooge but, once he has learned his part of the supposed Vincentio, he plays it with skill and gusto and his exchanges with the real Vincentio in Act 5, Scene 1 are hilarious. In the theatre when he pops his head out of the window, deadpans that he is Lucentio's father if his mother may be believed and tries to maintain the subterfuge that he is who he says he is, the audience is usually laughing delightedly. The actor frequently doubles up as the tailor so a good comedian is required.

Vincentio

Vincentio is a type of the returning absent parent seen in *Mostellaria* and other classical drama. He is not unduly affronted by the 'jest' of Katherine and Petruchio, pretending he is a 'young budding virgin' in Act 4, Scene 5 and wants to reward his travelling companions with a drink when they arrive in Padua. Vincentio is a good father wishing to surprise his son with a gift of 'a hundred pound or two to make merry' and is mortified when he thinks Lucentio has been murdered by Tranio for some nefarious enterprise. He is angry about the disguise plot but he is eventually talked round into agreeing to the secret marriage and praises Katherine for being 'toward' (compliant) during the feast in Act 5, Scene 2.

Target your thinking

- 'Language is the map of a character's mind.' Which language features, such as image clusters, does Shakespeare give to each of the main characters as the play develops? (**AO2**)

Form

The genre of *The Taming of the Shrew* is drama and to understand the play it is imperative that you have a sense of the play being performed in front of an audience, taking an interest in dramatic features such as soliloquy, aside, disguise, music, entrances, exits and which characters are on or off stage at key moments.

It is also hugely helpful to arrive at an understanding that the play is a script and on stage it can be interpreted and presented in a wide variety of ways. Production values are essential in drama as they will set the seal on what the director wants to present as key meanings. For example, Sly's concern for his unbroken English lineage is perhaps a peculiar thing for a horny-handed son of toil to be so bothered about but the play in performance will reveal things not visible on the page. Toby Frow's Globe production of 2012 began with Sly dressed in an England football shirt wandering drunkenly around Bankside accosting theatre-goers with a beer can in his hand. His lineage – linked to his football team – mattered to *this* manifestation of Sly.

Critics can have an impact on how a play is performed in the theatre: Nevill Coghill in *The Basis of Shakespearean Comedy*, calls Katherine a 'girl of spirit' who has 'developed the defensive technique of shrewishness', thus implicitly arguing that her shrewishness is a *disguise* to protect her from further hurt in a society which does not understand or value her. A good production may make use of Coghill's opinion and present Katherine as more self-consciously spirited than shrewish and more defensive than wild.

Structure

The play has a two-scene Induction, the only Shakespeare play to utilise this theatrical device. The theatre in Shakespeare's England was particularly detested by Puritans, who believed that it was a threat to God's order. In 1583's *Anatomy of Abuses*, Philip Stubbes refers to men who dress in women's clothing as 'monsters of both kinds, half women, half men'. The Induction deliberately and self-consciously draws attention to gender issues via Bartholomew dressing up as Sly's wife who is instructed to 'undress' and 'come to bed', making the audience focus on questions of male and female identity. Stubbes is disturbed

CRITICAL VIEW

Michael Bogdanov's 1978 Royal Shakespeare Company production utilised Sly as an audience member telling a female usher, 'No bloody woman pushes me about!' For Bogdanov the play is 'a male supremacist's fantasy, the longed-for revenge of the Sly clan on uppity women', arguing that the play represents 'the ruthless subduing of a woman … in a violent excess of male savagery' (cited in Hodgdon, 2010).

because the 'monstrous' image of a female character being played by a male has no essential nature as it has no essential gender. Males pretending to be women on stage mocked reality.

Plays by their very nature blur the lines of appearance and reality and perhaps *The Taming of the Shrew* blurs more lines than any other Shakespearean drama. The very structure of the play asks the audience willingly to suspend disbelief not once but several times. Consider being part of an audience coming to *Shrew* the first time with no prior knowledge of it. We know that the actors are not really the characters they are pretending to be on stage, so we will happily entertain the notion that *Shrew* is about Christopher Sly and the lord's attempt to make the drunken tinker believe he is an aristocrat. Then we see more actors troop on stage announcing that they are … actors. Next the lord (who we still know is an actor playing a lord) asks the actors pretending to be actors to stage a play for the benefit of a tinker whom we know to be an actor that the pretend lord is trying to convince is a real lord! When the play begins we see Sly watch the whole of the first scene and even hear from him before he slips out of sight at the changeover from Scene 1 to Scene 2. So, even if we aren't outraged Puritans like Stubbes, what are we watching? An elaborate practical joke played on a tinker? A play within a play? A satire? An early experiment in psychological theatre before the term psychology was coined? Directors who leave out the Induction remove at least one layer of potential meaning and perhaps make the play simpler but less elegant and far less intriguing.

The theme of appearance versus reality so dramatically constructed in the Induction features just as strikingly in the play proper: is Petruchio trying to save the 'real' Katherine from her unhappy early self? Is he a bully trying to teach her a lesson in obedience, conformity and real life? Anyway, what is his 'real' self when the Induction has set him up as a character played by an actor pretending to be an actor? What are we to make of it, as is common when directors include the Induction, if the same actor plays Sly and Petruchio? Who are the real Lucentio and the real Tranio?

Some feminist criticism argues that the Induction sets up Bartholomew as a 'woman' conforming to male stereotypes as a method of introducing Katherine in the play proper as a representative of a real woman trapped by the unfair expectations of a patriarchal society that uses women either as objects of sexual gratification, drudges or bargaining chips in the financial power games played by men. Critics with Marxist sympathies, such as Natasha Korda and Lena Orlin, point out that, though this feminist critique is undoubtedly true, the aristocrats with their overpowering sense of entitlement are ordering *everybody* – men *and* women – about. No one except the ruling class has any self-determinism. Self-identity and subjectivity are connected to possessions and class distinctions. The lord starts an experiment in the Induction and we don't even get to know how it ends: in no other play does Shakespeare leave the audience with so many choices about what the play means. Even Sly, the regular customer of 'Marian Hacket the fat ale-wife of Wincot', and drinking partner of 'John Naps' and

'Peter Turph' (who all seem very real and part of Warwickshire life which even had a Sly family in Stratford) begins to doubt his identity as his grasp on reality slips and he begins to believe in the new appearance of his life:

> Do I dream? Or have I dream'd till now?
> I do not sleep. I see, I hear, I speak.
> I smell sweet savours and I feel soft things.
> Upon my life I am a lord indeed,
> And not a tinker nor Christopher Sly.
>
> (Induction, Scene 2)

The play's structure sets up some intriguing and exciting possibilities of meaning.

Language

Much of the language of the play revolves around money: the discussions of financial arrangements witnessed in Act 1, Scene 1 are replayed in Act 1, Scene 2 with Petruchio's claim about his motives for seeking a bride. Yet is Petruchio's ebullience real or an act? He says wealth is a 'burden' of his 'wooing dance': burden in the late 1590s had a double meaning: one was a musical accompaniment and the second, more usual meaning was a heavy load. Which emphasis is Shakespeare making Petruchio stress in this context? Is he gleefully marching to the beat of monetary gain or does he find the whole business of negotiations burdensome? Perhaps there is a middle ground: he joyously swaggers towards the prospect of meeting a woman believed to be 'shrewd and froward beyond all measure' by the insipid and colourless merchants and brokers who shun and are afraid of her.

In Padua, peopled as it is with merchants like Baptista, dull nonentities like Hortensio, decrepit pantaloons like Gremio and moonstruck youths like Lucentio, the arrival of Petruchio has the impact of a full-sailed man-of-war peppering a sleepy fishing village with cannon fire. Much of the language of the play shows the differences between observers and doers. Petruchio's confession that he would 'fain be doing' confirms his energy. In his own account of his autobiography in Act 1, Scene 2, he is a force of nature who has experienced roaring lions, angry boars and neighing warhorses. He can outface thunderous tempests and stands firm and soldierly in the teeth of the cannon's roar and all the noises of the battlefield. Is it in any way likely that this macho roisterer will be put off by a woman's sharp tongue? Some may interpret Petruchio's speech as belittling the impact of women, by reducing the importance of their opinions symbolised by their tongues, symbolic of language at all levels, but the speech is perhaps best understood by placing it into the context of what Petruchio makes of the Paduans' report of Katherine rather than what *he* makes of Katherine, whom he has not yet even met.

The auction for Bianca in Act 2, Scene 1 continues the monetary theme and is conducted in a childish, boastful atmosphere: Gremio has a 'city house richly furnished with silver and gold, basins, ewers, hangings, ivory coffers stuffed with crowns, costly apparel, tents, canopies, fine linen, Turkey cushions' embossed 'with pearl', 'Venetian valances' picked out with gold thread, then rather more prosaically describes his farm with its 'hundred milch-kine' and 'six score fat oxe'. Tranio tries to trump Gremio with 'three or four houses in Pisa and two thousand ducats a year'. Gremio has now to up the stakes and confesses that he has an argosy in Marseilles but Tranio wins the auction by claiming his father has 'three great argosies, two galliases' and 'twelve galleys'. Little more than a list of possessions, the auction shows us how Bianca is regarded not as a person but how prized she is as a commodity and how expensive she is.

The speed with which Hortensio abandons Bianca in Act 4, Scene 2 – a woman who was his 'treasure' and the 'jewel of his life' in Act 1, Scene 2 – to focus his energies on the widow conveys his shallowness and transparency. That this waverer thinks he will be able to follow Petruchio's path and tame his widow is a sign of his delusional ignorance about his own nature. There is another verbal echo from earlier in the play when Hortensio calls Bianca a 'haggard', reflecting Petruchio's language of the previous scene. He may be able to use some of Petruchio's words but he lacks any of Petruchio's alpha-male qualities to convert those words into dynamic action. There is more than a whiff of Hortensio seeking to fortune-hunt here in the way he believes Petruchio has by his use of the adjective 'wealthy' to describe the widow. The clues are already here that he will fail.

Katherine's language is devoid of references to money and wealth and moves from its early stridency and threats to a measured and carefully constructed playfulness. Her acknowledgement in Act 4, Scene 5 that 'What you will have it named, even that it is, / And so it shall be so for Katherine' can be interpreted as a weary concession in the sun/moon argument which in itself is a continuation of the 'time of the day' argument begun in Act 4, Scene 3. However, Katherine's language to Vincentio has a gamesome quality which indicates she is enjoying the 'jest': her language is self-consciously courtly and mannered: 'Young budding virgin, fair, and fresh, and sweet, / Whither away, or where is thy abode?' The overly formal wording has clearly been 'composed' for the occasion to enhance the joke. To mistake an old man for a young maid is unnatural and therefore a type of unnatural, hyperbolic language is used in a spirit of playfulness. A broken-spirited, defeated woman would neither have the energy nor the motivation to play along with such gusto. The imagery of the sun and moon is important: in mythology the female moon 'followed' the male sun and mirrored its behaviour and the audience sees this celestial model re-enacted in the human world of Katherine and Petruchio. Katherine is in public here, in front of a stranger, a situation we know she finds difficult but she enters into Petruchio's spirit of things and is praised by Vincentio who calls her 'merry'. The last time she was in a public forum overlooked by strangers was in Act 1, Scene 1 when Tranio described her scolding behaviour as raising up such 'a storm that mortal ears might hardly endure the din' and of being 'curst' and 'shrewd'. Katherine is in a better place now because Shakespeare's language tells us so.

Even when Petruchio is merely giving directions as he does with Vincentio in Act 5, Scene 1, Shakespeare ensures his robust masculine nature is revealed through his speech – he tells Vincentio that Baptista's house 'bears' close to the marketplace. In using this nautical verb Shakespeare provides yet another clue about Petruchio's vigorous, piratical personality. Money is still close to the heart of the action: not only does Baptista symbolically live near the commercial hub of the city, Vincentio brings with him a 'hundred pound or two' for his son 'to make merry'. The casual, rich opulence of Lucentio and Vincentio is highlighted through the references to Tranio's borrowing Lucentio's 'pearls and gold'. In Act 4, Scene 2 the pedant informed us that, though he did not know Vincentio of Pisa personally, he had heard that he was 'a merchant of incomparable wealth'. Lucentio's confidence at the end of the scene that all will be well perhaps springs from his sense of entitlement as a member of a super-rich cosmopolitan elite.

Shakespeare shows how Petruchio and Katherine grow closer through their language, the map of a character's mind. That the exchange between Katherine and Petruchio which ends Act 5, Scene 1 is playful and affectionate is revealed through Shakespeare's language choices: Katherine calls Petruchio 'husband' and 'love'. This is the first time the audience has seen the couple kiss. We only heard about his 'comedy kiss' during the wedding when he was exaggerating his behaviour. Now, without irony, Petruchio calls his wife 'sweet Kate' after summing up that the situation is going 'well' and so we presume that all now will end well. What kind of kiss it is will depend on the director: in Zeffirelli's film Katherine gives Petruchio an innocent and somewhat motherly peck on the nose. In Toby Frow's Globe production it is a genuinely, romantic kiss; in Miller's BBC production it is a sexual kiss and Katherine and Petruchio lovingly whisper their next lines. The actors' voices and register will reveal much here: if Petruchio still hectors and Katherine is still strident, the scene will not work as romance. However, if their voices are calm and measured and thereby different from their earlier manic delivery – as they are in Zeffirelli, Frow and Miller – the audience will be able to see unequivocally that love has indeed 'wrought a miracle', though ironically not for Lucentio and the ever-selfish Bianca. Shakespeare also switches the language from prose, moving Petruchio's and Katherine's exchange into rhyming couplets to show their new-found togetherness and mutual regard. Due to these linguistic features the audience knows that Katherine and Petruchio are not pretending and have found mutual respect and love, important in terms of what we are to make of the final scene.

In the final scene Shakespeare once again utilises hunting and hawking images but another key idea is that once again marriage is linked to financial concerns.

Petruchio ups the ante: quintupling Lucentio's opening bid of 20 crowns. The language used by the husbands in trying to get their new wives to come is revealing: Lucentio 'bids', Hortensio 'entreats' and Petruchio 'commands'. Only a commanding, active and virile man, so it is implied, can hope to make a woman respect him enough to ensure that she is compliant and respectful.

Build critical skills

Choose a scene or two and decide what type of imagery dominates each one; for example, money, marriage, imagery around animals or insanity. Then track which characters Shakespeare links to each type of imagery and why.

Target your thinking

- How can analysing *The Taming of the Shrew* within a broad range of contexts deepen your understanding of the text and the ways in which different audiences might respond to it? (**AO3**)

Literary sources

Other than Plautus' *Mostellaria*, there is another direct literary source for the sub-plot in which Lucentio changes places with Tranio to win Bianca: this is George Gascoigne's 1573 English version of *The Supposes* based on Ludovico Ariosto's Italian *I Suppositi* (1551), itself based on early Greek and Roman models. In *I Suppositi*, Erostrato falls in love with Polynesta. Erostrato disguises himself as Dulipo, a servant, while the real servant Dulipo pretends to be Erostrato. Having done this, Erostrato is hired as a tutor for Polynesta. Meanwhile, Dulipo pretends to woo Polynesta so as to frustrate the wooing of the aged Cleander. Dulipo outbids Cleander, but he promises far more than he can deliver, so he and Erostrato dupe a travelling gentleman from Sienna into pretending to be Erostrato's father, Philogano, and to guarantee the dowry. Soon after, the real Philogano arrives and all comes to a head. Shakespeare utilises the plot of *I Suppositi* and inserts it wholesale as the sub-plot of *The Taming of the Shrew* and he keeps the name Petruchio, which he found in Gascoigne's version.

The Taming of a Shrew

The Taming of the Shrew and *The Taming of a Shrew* are clearly related. The main 'taming' plot is the same in both, and both have a sub-plot of romance and intrigue; Christopher Sly appears in both plays; the 'shrew' is tamed in both by very similar means conducted by Ferando in one and Petruchio in the other. In both plays the husband behaves scandalously at the wedding, starves his wife afterwards, rejects the work of a haberdasher and a tailor, and misuses his servant. In both the wife is transformed, asserts that the sun is the moon and pretends an old man is a young girl. Each play culminates in a feast at which men wager on their wives' obedience.

Shakespeare omits and changes some key details from his sources. In *I Suppositi* Erostrato gets Polynesta pregnant. Bianca might be duplicitous but she does not surrender her honour before marriage. In *A Shrew* Katherine is only ever Kate and the wooing scene to which Shakespeare devotes 97 lines is a mere 16 lines long. Clearly *A Shrew* is far less sophisticated in psychological terms than Shakespeare's play. Perhaps the most obvious alteration is Shakespeare's

Build critical skills

What does the audience lose and gain from Shakespeare's decision not to return to Sly at the conclusion of *The Taming of the Shrew*?

refusal to conclude the Induction with a return to Sly at the play's conclusion. In *A Shrew* Sly is dumped where he was found and upon waking imagines he has had the 'best dream' he has ever had and he will now go home and tame his wife. Given the many similarities between both plays it seems beyond doubt that Shakespeare was aware of *The Taming of a Shrew* and therefore beyond doubt his decision not to return to Sly was a conscious and deliberate one. Some critics are annoyed that Shakespeare does not 'close off' the Induction; others are delighted that the open ending leaves the audience with the potential to make their own meaning and helps create a sense of wonder.

The oral tradition

Extremely strong oral traditions about powerful women and shrew-taming survive in various societies across the world. We have already seen that the Induction scene was inspired by the English folk song 'The Frolicsome Duke' (see p. 6). A ballad, 'A Merry Jest of a Shrewd and Curst Wife', in which the husband beats his wife and wraps her in the salted skin of a dead horse was so popular it was printed in 1550. Here was a tale of wife-taming cruelty Shakespeare did not bring with him into *The Taming of the Shrew* as it lacked any kind of psychological depth and was crude in the extreme.

Jan Harold Brunvand (born March 23, 1933) is an American folklorist, and long-time Emeritus Professor of English at the University of Utah, most famous for codifying and bringing to public attention the concept of the urban myth, a form of modern folklore. In 1961, Brunvand received a PhD in Folklore from Indiana University. His dissertation, '*The Taming of the Shrew* : A Comparative Study of Oral and Literary Versions (Aarne-Thompson type 901)' highlighted his interest in the development and importance of the folktale. Brunvand's research into various versions of the play is revealing: his detailed analysis of 'tale type' reveals a narrative that occurs throughout India and Europe, presenting a compelling map of features of *The Taming of the Shrew*'s plot against traditions of oral legacy. Brunvand finds 35 literary or written versions of the 'taming tale' and 383 oral versions from 30 different countries or ethnic or national groups. Within the oral tradition Brunvand finds eleven areas of commonality:

1 The taming is a play within a play or story within a story. In *The Taming of the Shrew* we see this in the Induction scenes.
2 The shrew is usually the elder of two daughters, as we see in Act 1, Scene 1, and is identified with the devil. See how Gremio and Hortensio compare Katherine to the devil and the devil's dam.
3 The father is rich and warns the prospective suitor about the shrew's nature, offering a large dowry. In the play we see this feature in Act 1, Scene 2 and in Act 2, Scene 1.
4 The suitor is confident he can tame the shrew and places a bet that he can do so. We see Petruchio's confidence in Act 2, Scene 2 but he does not make a bet here; Shakespeare waits until Act 5, Scene 2.

5 The groom arrives late for the wedding service, is dressed inappropriately and rides an old horse. Often he has a falcon. He behaves in a boorish or bizarre fashion and refuses to stay before beginning the trip home during which the bride and groom ride on one horse or the husband rides, making the wife walk. We see this feature in Act 3, Scene 2 and in Act 4, Scene 1. Though Petruchio does not bring a falcon with him to the wedding, he uses falconry techniques to change Katherine's behaviour. Based on Grumio's story to Curtis in Act 4, Scene 1, we learn that Katherine and Petruchio have a horse each.

6 The taming occurs at the husband's home or on a trip to visit the wife's parents. The husband beats his servants and/or punishes or sometimes even kills his dog for a supposed fault as a warning to his wife. Petruchio 'tames' Katherine at his own home in Act 4, Scene 1, calls for his dog Troilus and does comically knock his servants about. Nathaniel comments that this is most unusual behaviour for Petruchio: 'didst ever see the like?'

7 There is a school where other husbands can learn the shrew-taming process. Hortensio goes to Petruchio's 'taming school' after he realises he has no chance of winning Bianca in Act 4, Scene 2.

8 Taming tactics include depriving the wife of food and getting her to agree to her husband's absurd statements: several tales include the husband calling the sun the moon and a man a woman. We see this in *The Taming of the Shrew* in Act 4, Scene 1 and Act 4, Scene 5.

9 The test of the wife's obedience takes place after dinner at the father-in-law's house. During this test the wife looks over some new clothes. The reward for the wife's obedience is a prize offered by the father-in-law. Shakespeare removes the link of the clothes and places it within Act 4, Scene 3, leaving the obedience test to Act 5, Scene 2 where he reintroduces the notion of the bet, which in the oral tradition comes earlier.

10 The wife comes immediately when called and is courteous. She throws her cap on the floor and steps on it, pulls off her husband's boots to clean them, places her hand under his foot, brings all the wives in to lecture them and kisses her husband. We see some but not all of these features in Act 5, Scene 2. Critics have been bothered for years about exactly where the notion of Katherine offering to place her hand under the foot of the husband comes from because it appears to have no literary source. However, the behaviour belongs to an oral and not a literary tradition.

11 Others characters conclude that the shrew's husband has won some form of victory. We see this in Act 5, Scene 2.

The sources for the play appear to be far more oral than literary. Therefore we can suggest that the story of a woman being tamed was already known to Shakespeare and his original audience through the oral tradition. Brunvand argues that Shakespeare's version of the story is distinctly English and that Shakespeare clearly knew the story from folklore, probably from his own native Warwickshire, so important in the Induction. However, Shakespeare's Petruchio deviates from the norm of the folklore tamer in that he allows his wife to ride her own horse and does not make her walk, and although she does fall from her horse into the mire, Petruchio has not stage-managed it. Petruchio is not cruel to his dogs and he does not kill a domestic animal as an example to his wife. Shakespeare's Petruchio may be 'one half lunatic, a madcap ruffian' but, unlike the folklore tamer, he is democratic about the transport, he practises relative forbearance in his examples of violence and does not retaliate to Katherine's violence with violence of his own.

Dowries and jointures

Petruchio: What dowry shall I have with her to wife?

Baptista: After my death the one half of my lands,
            And in possession twenty thousand ducats.

Petruchio: And for that dowry I'll assure her of
            Her widowhood be it that she survive me,
            In all my land and leases whatsoever.

(Act 2, Scene 1)

In Tudor England dowries were particularly important because they were a means of conferring status, and of transferring and redistributing wealth. A marriage would not be agreed unless a dowry was arranged. Dowries have frequently been misunderstood as merely a means whereby a potential husband could get his hands on a portion of his future wife's family's wealth but dowries could also safely cement the social position of women via their property rights. In the play the amounts discussed in Act 2, Scene 1 are astronomical for the era. Twenty thousand crowns converts to about £5,000 in the late sixteenth century. In a proclamation of 1587 regulating London wages, even the most skilled artisans — the brewers, cooks, butchers and blacksmiths — had their wages limited to £6 per annum. Petruchio is also remarkably generous in his offer of all his lands and leases going to Katherine upon his death. He may be 'wiving it wealthily' because he will get a one-off sum equivalent to 834 years' worth of work for a blacksmith but Katherine will get *all* his property and rent should he die before her. One wonders if Petruchio is not expecting children to result from his marriage to Katherine as it was usual for male heirs to inherit — or is he a proto-feminist, trusting Katherine to do the right thing by any children they have in the event of his predeceasing her? Are they considerably older than Lucentio and Bianca and may not expect to have children as a matter of course? Under Common Law, women were entitled to a 'lifetime of dower' of a third of their husband's freeholding during their widowhood, so Katherine is going to do uncommonly well out of this arrangement. One wonders what an Elizabethan audience would have made of such sums. Estimates vary about how much 20,000 ducats would be worth today but amounts of between £15–25 million have been calculated. In today's terms Baptista's dowry for Katherine is the equivalent of winning a very large pay-out on the EuroMillions lottery.

Increasingly from the late medieval period, marriage agreements specified the portion brought by the bride and, in return for her dowry, a settlement in the form of a 'jointure' to maintain her if her husband died first. The amount of a contractual jointure would usually be more than the third guaranteed under Common Law or if it were less it would be used to supplement the third. In one sense a jointure was a means whereby a caring family could 'pay forward' a sum for when their daughter needed it in the event of her widowhood. Money played a very important part in the process, even where the amounts endowed were not as large as they are in the play.

> Baptista: 'Tis deeds must win the prize, and he of both
>   That can assure my daughter greatest dower
>   Shall have my Bianca's love [...]
>
> Tranio: I'll leave her houses three or four as good
>   Within rich Pisa walls as any one
>   Old Signor Gremio has in Padua,
>   Besides two thousand ducats by the year
>   Of fruitful land, all which shall be her jointure.
>
> (Act 2, Scene 1)

Breaking all rules of marriage protocol, and as he himself admits 'I play a merchant's part / And venture madly on a desperate mart', Baptista asks the *men* what they will give as dowries to win Bianca. There can be no doubt that this is an auction. Perhaps Baptista needs to recoup the expenses promised to Petruchio. It is noticeable that though Baptista told Petruchio twice that a condition of the marriage was winning Katherine's love, Baptista makes no similar demand of the winner of the auction for Bianca's hand. As far as Baptista is concerned, Bianca's love for Gremio or 'Lucentio' does not come into it. It is therefore somewhat surprising that many critics argue that Baptista favours Bianca, when financially and in terms of securing her love before a marriage is agreed, Katherine clearly has the better of it. Tranio/Lucentio offers a dowry *and* a jointure, surely an unheard-of event for the original audience but something which may pass by unnoticed today. We can assume that Shakespeare's audience paid much closer attention to the details of Katherine's and Bianca's dowry and jointure than a modern audience. The wealth offered by Tranio as a dowry and for Bianca's jointure is eye-wateringly opulent, an offer only open to the super-rich.

Performance

This enigmatic play can be performed in widely different ways, having been presented as everything from a Western romp to a very dark tale of abuse and sexual cruelty.

TASK

Baptista's insistence that Petruchio must have Katherine's love has been explained as cynical, feeble or hypocritical. However, Baptista does say it, not once but twice. Importantly, in the auction for Bianca which concludes the scene, he does not mention the suitors having to get Bianca's love at all. Can it be thus inferred that Baptista actually favours Katherine over Bianca and is more concerned about Katherine's happiness than her sister's?

Build critical skills

Consider what your own ideal production of *The Taming of the Shrew* would be like in terms of ideas and staging. Draw ideas from productions you have seen or read about and make notes under headings like: *Period set in; Costume style; Ideas to emphasise; Critical stance.*

Film

The play has always been used as a vehicle for famous 'star' acting partnerships: Douglas Fairbanks and Mary Pickford began the tradition with a 1929 film, released just days before the Wall Street Crash. The Induction in the film includes a Punch-and-Judy-style puppet show at the end of which Judy falls into Punch's arms after he has 'swinged' her good and proper with his big stick. Freudians can have fun with that one. Fairbanks and Pickford were in the final stages of their marriage during filming and their off-screen relationship was as fiery as the one on-screen. The restored film has been recently uploaded onto YouTube and is well worth viewing. Katherine is never tamed and at each stage of the relationship she gives at least as good as she gets. Fairbanks' swashbuckling Petruchio, dressed like Zorro without his mask, is extremely dashing and he spends much of the film running up staircases and laughing heartily with a whip in his hand. Pickford's Katherine similarly brandishes a whip for much of the play which she uses freely on the other characters, especially Petruchio. During Katherine's final speech Petruchio is uncomprehending as he had been felled and rendered senseless by a hefty 'joint-stool' flung by Katherine in Act 4. Fairbanks' Petruchio mixes up the sun and moon quite literally as the bang on the head has affected his judgement. Significantly Katherine winks at Bianca during her final speech, showing that Katherine knows what she is saying is a joke and lets the audience in on it. Pickford's Katherine remains completely in charge throughout.

In 1963 John Wayne's production company Batjac financed a Western, based (loosely) on Shakespeare's play. *McLintock!* was released the same year as Betty Friedan's *The Feminine Mystique*, which galvanised the women's liberation movement, particularly in the USA.

Context

The Feminine Mystique (1963) describes what psychologist Friedan calls 'the problem with no name': the essential unhappiness of American housewives who do not feel fulfilled despite having lives of material comfort and children able to be brought up without poverty. Friedan criticises the theories of Sigmund Freud, the influence of media and particularly the role of advertising in promoting the myth that being a wife and mother will fulfil women's needs. Friedan recommends education and meaningful work as ways for women to avoid becoming trapped.

The film's promotional activities had to be postponed due to the assassination of President Kennedy but it was a box-office success nonetheless and gave Wayne's career a timely boost after a number of flops. A farcical romp with lots of Wayne's deeply conservative political views as well as some of his homespun Western libertarianism seeping through the cracks, the film appears quite at odds with the more liberal zeitgeist of the sixties. For example, Wayne insisted that the weak governor be called 'Cuthbert H. Humphrey', to parody Democrat Senator Hubert H. Humphrey, whom Wayne roundly detested. There is also a speech by Wayne's character, George Washington (G.W.) McLintock, the biggest landowner in the territory, given apparently in defence of the native Americans: 'If you knew anything about Indians, you'd know that they're doing their level best to put up with our so-called "benevolent patronage" in spite of the nincompoops that've been put in charge of it!' What G.W. doesn't address is why he owns all the land and the indigenous population are addicted to whiskey and living in poverty and squalor on the reservation. In a manner reminiscent of *Scooby-Doo* for low-achieving, low-ability adults, G.W. blames the meddlesome government. In Shakespeare's play Petruchio is not stupid. The film also contains two scenes of men putting women over their knees and spanking them with little coal shovels, one of which is the filmic climax when G.W. 'tames' his errant wife, dressed in nothing but her wet underwear, in front of the whole town. In many ways *McLintock!* is a strange film; things were different in the sixties.

The most famous married actors of the era were Elizabeth Taylor and Richard Burton who were cast by Franco Zeffirelli for his 1967 film adaptation.

Elizabeth Taylor is very watchable as Katherine who gives the final speech in an entirely serious manner, hands on hips, with no Pickfordesque winking. However, she leaves the banquet on her own and Petruchio has to go scampering after her. Petruchio is not entirely in command. Of her role, Taylor said that 'to control men, women have to pretend to obey them'. She had clearly thought about some of the complexities and challenges of playing Katherine but, in a case of art mimicking life, Burton plays Petruchio as a drunk, thereby losing much of Shakespeare's subtlety in characterisation. Far less subtle than even Burton's performance is the text of the publicity poster which seems to assume domestic violence is commonplace and that women deserve the 'back of the hand' from men who are struggling to control them.

10 Things I Hate About You is a thoughtful 1999 updating of the play set in and around Padua High School that sees Kat Stratford interact with rebel outsider Patrick Verona. It can be seen as a celebration of young American women, presenting them as shrewder, more intelligent and more moral than other films in the teen romance genre. The film's pleasures are many. Director Gil Younger and writers Karen McCullah Lutz and Kirsten Smith allow their teenagers their naivety and doubts but also give them a gentle and tender nobility which makes them charmingly human. Kat, beautifully played by Julia Stiles, is different to other teen heroines and does not want to conform. In her unconventionality and initial unhappiness she is clearly reminiscent of Shakespeare's Katherine. Like Shakespeare's original comedy where genre dictates outcome, Kat and Patrick, given a quirky anti-formulaic swagger by Heath Ledger, find mutual understanding and respect in a happy ending.

Context

The publicity text in the middle of one version of the poster advertising the Burton and Taylor adaptation reads: 'A motion picture for every man who ever gave the back of his hand to his beloved … and for every woman who deserved it. Which takes in a lot of people!' Burton and Taylor produced this film, invested over a million dollars and worked for nothing on it, electing instead to take a percentage of the profits. It made $12 million. Have a look at the advertising posters online.

▲ Kat and Patrick from *10 Things I hate About You* (1999)

Stage

Fairbanks' and Pickford's fireworks when making the 1929 film quickly became Hollywood legend and in 1935 Lynn Fontanne and Alfred Lunt, another feuding married couple, played the main roles on Broadway for a record 129 performances before embarking on a hugely popular US tour. Fontanne and Lunt were responsible for the 'scheme of the production', meaning they were the real directors, not Harry Gribble who got the credit in the programme. This production was an out-and-out farce involving trained animals and other circus performers, including acrobats and dwarves, and the actors would often stop the action and involve the audience in the play.

TASK

To what extent do you agree with the notion that the term 'farce' is a satisfactory description of the play as a whole?

Context

Farce is a sub-genre of comedy in which buffoonery, clowning, improbable situations, absurdities and crude characterisation are deliberately used to inculcate laughter in the audience. In modern French 'une farcie' is a crêpe stuffed with finely minced meat and/or mushrooms. The idea derives from early modern theatre when purely comic and absurd sections of low humour and horseplay were 'stuffed' into more serious texts.

This clever trick maintained the spirit of the Induction for well into the first act as latecomers would be heckled by the actors on some nights while on others the actors would stop the action and explain to the tardy patrons what they had missed and how entertaining the show was or how good the acting had been. Coughing in the audience could lead to the entire cast breaking into fits of coughing, sneezing or rolling about the stage pretending they were dying. The production seems to have been wild and zany, with Katherine's and Petruchio's last exit seeing them ascending up into the gods in a golden chariot, accompanied by choral music, indicating a camp Broadway version of marital heaven. However, the production was not all kitsch: the directors were cleverly sympathetic to some of the play's more serious themes. Early Katherine is invisible and off stage during Act 1, Scene 1, her lines shouted from the wings accompanied by her flinging objects at the on-stage performers, an idea 'borrowed' from the 1929 film. Fontanne's temper and mood with Lunt would dictate the accuracy, type, force and number of objects being hurled on stage on any given night. Such inter-marital strife on and off the set of *Shrew* upstaged even the Fairbankses and became so legendary that Cole Porter's 1948 musical *Kiss Me, Kate*, about a fiery couple attempting to stage an adaptation of *The Taming of the Shrew*, was based on Fontanne's and Lunt's off-stage performances.

▲ All-male Old Vic production of *The Taming of the Shrew* (Edward Hall 2007)

At the complete opposite end of the spectrum, Charles Marowitz's 'free adaption' *The Shrew*, which toured internationally in 1975, was deliberately provocative, highlighting what Marowitz saw as the essential ugliness of the play in which Katherine suffers outrageous cruelties at the hands of her savage husband, culminating in anal rape. She mutters her final speech robotically in an asylum-style robe, prompted throughout by Petruchio who has reduced her to a cipher, a shadow, a ghost of her former self. In Marowitz's redesigned gothic horror, the Induction was omitted, the characters of Gremio and Hortensio were removed, and the Bianca/Lucentio sub-plot featured as a modern-day parallel story, with both characters being anonymous representatives of modern men and women. Marowitz also removed all aspects of comedy, and rearranged much of the Shakespeare dialogue he did keep, for example moving Bartholomew's 'Sly's wife's speech' about abstaining from sex from the Induction to the dénouement and giving it to Katherine, thus becoming the speech which provokes the rape. The final image of the play is Katherine in a wedding dress, chained to the ground, as a funeral bell tolls. Marowitz described his intention in *The Shrew* as 'an attempt to test or challenge, revoke or destroy the intellectual foundation which makes "a classic" the formidable thing it has become [and to] combat the assumptions of "a classic" with a series of new assumptions, and force it to bend under the power of a new polemic' (cited in Holderness, 1989). Marowitz presents Petruchio as a psychopathic, misogynistic rapist. We may question whether this is artistically justified. *The Taming of the Shrew* is a comedy and consequently it does not include rape. This is not to say that Shakespeare did not portray rape elsewhere in his work. He wrote the poem *The Rape of Lucrece* (1594) and rape features prominently in his play *Titus Andronicus* (circa 1592/3) in which the characters Chiron and Demetrius, egged on by their mother Tamora, rape Lavinia and, to prevent her revealing the crime or their identities, they cut out her tongue and cut off her hands so she cannot even write their names. Shakespeare was not afraid to write of horrific cruelty and to do so in graphic detail but it is a fact that he did not do so in *The Taming of the Shrew*.

If an audience were to watch *McLintock!*, *10 Things I Hate About You* and *The Shrew* back to back, other than from the clue in Marowitz's title, it is unlikely that they would place Shakespeare's version as the pivotal play around which all three productions revolve.

Historical context

Tudor ideas about power

Tudor writers, especially from the 1570s to the end of Elizabeth's reign, became intrigued by notions of kingship, monarchy, supremacy, order and the acquisition and retention of power, particularly when judged against ideas of virtue in civic and military matters. Shakespeare seems always to have been interested in these ideas and in such plays as *Richard II*, *Richard III*, *Julius Caesar*, *Coriolanus* and *Troilus and Cressida* he explores ideas concerning power and governance. However, notions of female power, male reactions to it, supremacy, lawful rule and peaceful society are also fully explored in early comedies such as *The Taming of the Shrew* which, despite its many and frequent realistic touches, can also be considered as a domestic allegory of a male-female power struggle played out at the very top political levels of society: female power was a very important matter in Elizabethan England.

Tudor intellectuals saw the role of the monarch to be both self-limiting and self-regulating; a good ruler was bound by reason, duty and honour not to exceed the

Taking it further ▷

Is it fair to Shakespeare's original vision of the play that Charles Marowitz turns Petruchio into a sadistic rapist? How does Marovitz's interpretation add to our understanding of Shakespeare's play? Research how other productions present Petruchio.

limits of his power and always to act in the public good. Within the *domus* the patriarch was meant to represent the model of a good ruler as a household was an entire society in microcosm. Thomas Aquinas defined a tyrant as a ruler who ruled for his own profit rather than for the good of all. Aristotle's third book of the *Politics* had argued against the legitimacy of a monarchy based solely on the will of the sovereign. The blind will of a monarch could only be held in check by what the Romans termed '*amicitia*', a blanket term that covered many things from what we today would understand as friendship to the liberty of something approaching free speech whereby a counsellor gave 'honest opinion' which the ruler received in a spirit of generosity and equality. The equality was to some degree illusory: in Henry VIII's court, butcher's son Wolsey was not of equal social status to the king – not even when he was appointed cardinal – but the king presumed (or pretended to assume) *amicitia* within the Privy Council, conferring upon his advisers the trust that they were the king's 'friends' who were to act as his 'eyes, ears and feet', helping him rule justly and securing his power. In Henry's reign the notion seldom worked. To be a privy councillor or among Henry's intimate circle was extremely dangerous. Henry planned to execute Wolsey who died before he could stand trial and did execute Sir Thomas More and Thomas Cromwell as well as dozens of other prominent public figures. Some historians estimate that he had 72,000 executed during his reign – hardly the Renaissance Humanist ideal.

Queen Elizabeth, the symbolism of female power and the play

The idea of a bountiful relationship between ruler and the ruled and of *amicitia* between monarch and advisers lies at the heart of Queen Elizabeth's reign. Though Elizabeth did execute religious intransigents, she did not murder her councillors in the cruelly erratic manner or in anything like the huge numbers her father did. The harmonious ideal of reason and good governance can, perhaps, be best seen in one of the most famous and iconic images of Elizabeth's reign in the 'Rainbow Portrait'. The portrait, commissioned by Robert Cecil in 1600 and finished in 1602 (which hangs in Hatfield House) is a masterpiece of Tudor allegory: the ears and eyes that adorn the queen's gown may represent her privy councillors who, like her father's council, were the eyes and ears who watch and listen, but do not speak.

Context

William Cecil (1520-1598), first Baron Burghley was Queen Elizabeth's chief adviser. He was succeeded by his son Robert (1563-1612) who was extensively involved in matters of state security. As a protégé of Sir Francis Walsingham (Elizabeth's principal spymaster), he was an expert in intelligence and codes. The clearly allegorical 'Rainbow portrait' may relate to this role. Robert Cecil, like his father, greatly admired the queen, whom he described as being 'more than a man, but less than a woman'.

On the one hand the portrait shows ever-youthful Gloriana in her majestic splendour but – if we take the symbolism as primarily Aristotelian – it is also an icon of a limited, i.e. a non-tyrannical, monarchy. Other interpretations of the portrait are available but all revolve around the importance of allegorical symbolism.

ON SINE SOLE
IRIS.

▲ Historian Frances Yates cites Cesare Ripa's *Iconologia* of 1593, a popular handbook of symbols, allegories and emblems, as the key to the portrait's meanings. To Yates the eyes and ears on her cloak symbolise Elizabeth's fame, which is flying through the world, seen and heard by multitudes

In the portrait, Elizabeth stands before a dark archway holding in her right hand a rainbow above which is inscribed the Latin motto '*NON SINE SOLE IRIS*': 'no rainbow without a sun'. The rainbow, which comes after storms, signifies serenity and peace. Petruchio praises the importance of domestic peace in Act 5, Scene 2 when he interprets the meaning of Katherine's appearance in symbolic terms: 'Marry, peace it bodes, and love and quiet life / An awful rule and right supremacy'. Elizabeth is the sun: the centre of all. With her left hand she touches the hem of her ornate cloak, decorated with human eyes and ears. Shakespeare makes much use of the sun and the moon during Petruchio's and Katherine's journey back to visit Baptista in Act 5, Scene 1, in which Petruchio insists that his world view is superior to hers.

The queen's left sleeve is decorated with a bejewelled serpent just above which is an armillary sphere (an astrolabe or model of the visible heavens constructed from rings and hoops representing the equator, the tropics, and other celestial circles, and able to revolve on its axis) encircled by a 'zodiac band' representing planets and star signs. Elizabeth was celestially ordained. The serpent represents prudence, vigilance and intelligence – both personal and political. The queen's bodice is decorated with flowers, three pearl necklaces, several bracelets, and a cruciform brooch. The floral decoration on the bodice shows pansies, honeysuckles and cowslips. Pansies, from the French '*pensée*', symbolise thoughtfulness, honeysuckles signify sweet happiness and love and the cowslips (primroses) signify the beautiful mystery of the Holy Trinity (from the medieval era) and from *Henry V* good management. If we combine the two meanings we see that the portrait signifies the church is being well governed.

The pearls symbolise virginity and the jewelled crescent *moon* in the head-dress links to Diana, Roman goddess of virginity and hunting, signifying Elizabeth the chaste, watchful warrior bringing light to the world and her kingdom. Petruchio compares Katherine to Diana in Act 2, Scene 1, lines 260 to 263 and for the whole play she is a virgin, her marriage not yet consummated when the couple make their final exit in Act 5, Scene 2.

The queen is also adorned by a gauze transparent veil and an elaborate lace-embroidered collar of remarkable size which, to many observers, takes on the appearance of wings. Despite all of her magnificence, her angelic grandeur and her portrait dripping in symbolism, she is a transparent and open ruler. Art historian Roy Strong comments, 'The visual arts retreated in favour of presenting a series of signs or symbols through which the viewer was meant to pass to an understanding of the idea behind the work. In this manner the visual arts were verbalised, turned into a form of book, a "text" which called for reading by the onlooker' (1999).

Symbolism was hugely important for Elizabethans and the queen herself was well aware of her symbolic importance: the supreme governor was 'authorised' immediately by God; disobedience to the monarch was ultimately disobedience to God. In Katherine's last speech she gives a sermon on how disobedience to the honest will of a husband is tantamount to treason on the wife's part and by extension disobedience of God's laws.

There was always a gender conflict at the heart of Elizabethan government which was played out in a politico-religious battle of the sexes. Elizabeth had been made nervous by the rule of Queen Mary who had been attacked by extremist Protestants on the grounds of religion and gender. Her religious enemies categorised Catholic Mary as the Jezebel of the Bible, the wife of Ahab, King of Israel, who had encouraged the worship of Baal and tried to destroy the prophets of Israel (I Kings 18:4–13). That Jezebel had been thrown out of an upper window by eunuchs, trampled underfoot by Jehu's horses and her corpse consumed by dogs (II Kings 9:29–37) gave Mary's Protestant detractors scriptural authority to call for her murder. Much of the hatred aimed at Mary was anti-female.

John Knox wrote perhaps the most misogynistic text in European history with his *First Blast of the Trumpet against the Monstrous Regiment of Women* (1559) in which he rants, 'To promote a woman to bear rule, superiority, dominion or empire above any realm, nation or city is repugnant to nature, contumely to God, a thing most contrarious to His revealed will and approved order, and finally it is the subversion of good order, of all equity and justice … How abominable before God is the empire or rule of a wicked woman, yea, of a traiteresse and bastard.' Hortensio and Gremio talk of Katherine in terms reminiscent of Puritan frames of reference: Katherine is a 'devil', 'the devil's dam' and marriage to her would be akin to being sent to 'hell'. Even Baptista refers to her 'devilish spirit'. Furthermore, in Knox's world a female ruler was a 'monster in nature'. Elizabeth was livid when the polemic appeared unaltered shortly after her accession but Knox was unmoved. He did not care that Elizabeth was a Protestant and Mary had been a Catholic. Elizabeth was not an extreme Protestant of the sort that Knox admired and, according to his extremist logic, as a woman Elizabeth should not be in any position of authority anyway.

Aware of the accusations that Mary was Jezebel, Queen Elizabeth's coronation rituals and pageants were constructed around the notion that she was a new and symbolic Deborah, ushering in a new epoch of goodness.

Context

Deborah in the Old Testament was a prophetess and the 'judge and restorer' of Israel who defeated the Canaanites and delivered the people of Israel (Judges 4-5). However, it would seem that stereotypes of gender were so deeply engrained into the Tudor psychology that even Mary's death and the coronation of the 'English Deborah' continued a sense of the anxiety that female monarchy created.

Elizabeth's reign – whether she consciously constructed it so, or due to the constraints of being a female ruler – saw more power go to the Privy Council than had been the case in the reigns of Henry VII and Henry VIII. Under Elizabeth, the Privy Council issued proclamations, regulated the poor laws, set prices and wages in London, and advised justices of the peace on wages in other parts of the country. It even controlled vagrancy of the kind that Sly temporarily exemplifies in the Induction when he is sleeping in a ditch.

Marriage: Petruchio the anarchic bridegroom?

Context

The word 'wedding' comes from the Old English *weddian* – 'to pledge oneself'; 'marriage' enters English via the Old French then the Norman French word *mariage*, meaning the entry into wedlock. It is interesting to note that in its earlier uses *mariage* also meant *dowry*.

Handfasting

Pre-medieval married couples would pledge each other in a cup of wine and in many medieval and early modern European societies a 'handfasting' ceremony or pledge was usually sufficient to bind the bargain. Marriages made by vows of betrothal were valid and legal as long as they had been witnessed by others. In Shakespeare's late tragi-comedy *The Winter's Tale*, young lovers Florizel and Perdita are prevented by Polixenes, Florizel's father in disguise, from entering into a **handfast** marriage. In medieval England handfast marriages were essentially the only kind of marriage available to ordinary people because formalised weddings conducted inside a church were the sole preserve of the aristocracy.

handfasting: is a historical term for a betrothal or a marriage brought into Old English via the Old Norse term *handfesta* meaning "to strike a bargain by joining hands".

Context

Handfasted marriages involved the joining of the bride's and groom's hands, as well as a public exchange of vows known as 'troth-plight' (in modern English, a 'trust-pledge', i.e. a promise to be trustworthy and faithful). Much literature of the era is concerned with troth-plights which were much more popular with young lovers than their parents who were likely to have been far more concerned with the financial and political side to marriage than their loved-up children.

However, handfasting was an imperfect system because the marriages were oral transactions; though deeply serious because they were taken under oath, they left no formal written trace. If the witnesses died or moved away handfasted marriages became more part of local folklore than public record. Even, as was often the case, one of the witnesses had been the local priest and the 'ceremony' had been conducted outside of the church door or in the porch, again as was common, it was always extremely difficult and often impossible to keep track of who had married whom, and where and when the event had occurred.

During Shakespeare's life the number of handfast marriages began to concern church officials and parents, who were not always informed of handfast marriages. It was about this time that handfast ceremonies came to signify betrothal rather than marriage. Unlike marriage, which now had to be sanctioned officially by the church, handfast betrothals were not indissoluble; nevertheless, handfasts did involve commitment and formal intent to marry. They also presumed that troth-plight sanctioned sexual intimacy. In *The Winter's Tale* Leontes, King of Sicilia, in the middle of a jealous rant about his wife Hermione's presumed (but completely unfounded) infidelity, says:

> *My wife's a hobby-horse, deserves a name*
>
> *As rank as any flax-wench that puts to*
>
> *Before her troth-plight.*

The implication is that it is morally acceptable – even for a lowly flax-wench – to have sex (to 'put to' – the sense lingers in the American phrase to 'put out') *after* troth-plight but not before. The tradition of handfast marriages was falling into disrepute especially for townspeople from the early sixteenth century. One common reason given was that they had become a way of licentious young men to seduce women only to leave them after they had enjoyed their sexual pleasures. In 1530 Richard Whitford wrote, 'Many men when they cannot obtain their unclean desire of the woman will promise marriage, and thereupon make a contract promise saying, "Here I take thee Margery unto my wife, I thereto plight thee my troth." And she again, unto him in like manner. And after that done, they suppose they may lawfully use their unclean behaviour, and sometime the act and deed doth follow' (*A Work for Householders*). More scandalous still was the case of Anne Boleyn's secret handfasting to Lord Henry Percy in 1523 when only direct involvement from Cardinal Wolsey, the Duke of Northumberland (Percy's father) and Henry VIII himself put an end to the 'marriage'.

The kiss at the altar

Kissing in public to seal formal attachments appears to have developed in Tours, France, in the sixth century, when fashionable young men began to give rings to their betrothed as a symbol that they were bound to them. In addition, a pair of shoes, to indicate male subjection to the female was given (see below), and a kiss on the lips given as proof of love. Gradually the kiss at the altar entered the wedding service. Petruchio makes a big event of drinking wine which he 'quaffed off' before throwing sops in the sexton's face. Sops were pieces of wine-soaked bread or cake traditionally given to wedding guests. 'This done, he took the bride about the neck / And kissed her lips with such a clamorous smack' (Gremio, Act 3, Scene 2). It seems that Petruchio is self-consciously playing a part with his disruptive behaviour during his wedding ceremony.

The vows

The vows were slightly different for men and women in the Elizabethan wedding service. Unlike today, couples could not choose their own wedding vows and needed to abide by the form of words laid out in the Book of Common Prayer of 1549. Thus it was that the husband vowed to 'love, comfort, honour, and keep his wife in sickness and in health, forsaking all others'. In return, the wife promised to 'obey, serve, love, honour, keep in sickness and in health, forsaking all others'. The vow was binding up to death. The words spoken at the end of an Elizabethan marriage were very different to today: 'Saint Peter also doth instruct you very godly, thus saying, "Let wives be subject to their own husbands, so that if any obey not the word, they may be won without the word, by the conversation of the wives."' Clearly the term 'conversation' has its own unique sixteenth-century meaning and most scholars translate it as 'behaviour'. We have an additional problem in that the religious Tudor English used in the Book of Common Prayer is a little convoluted for an entirely clear modern understanding. However, we can discern a hint here that if words alone do not make a wife conformable, then certain patterns of behaviour will. Petruchio's behaviour is certainly more instructive and successful in its impact on Katherine than his words alone.

Marriage by capture

'Marriage by capture' is categorised in the European Union as a sex crime but in ancient times it was a practice whereby women were abducted for the purpose of marriage. Anthropologists aver it is still conducted today in Africa, Central Asia, the Caucasus, East and South Asia and South America.

Context

A relic of 'marriage by capture' may *allegedly* be seen in modern Britain and Ireland in the Romany-Traveller tradition of a young man 'grabbing' a young woman at weddings and demanding a kiss. This ritual involves the young man using some physical coercion upon the female. Television footage exists purporting to illustrate 'grabbing', though many travellers have claimed recently that it is a complete fiction entirely invented for the Channel 4 series *My Big Fat Gypsy Wedding*.

If two men were attracted to the same woman, the one who won her hand might first have to win a competition of physical prowess. Chaucer explores this idea in the pitched battle fought by Palamon and Arcite in *The Knight's Tale*. Much 'quest literature' stems from the notion that men have to 'prove themselves' to women and their families. Importantly, in early modern and nascent capitalist societies it could be argued that marriage by capture was replaced by a new form of 'marriage by purchase' – essentially what we see in Padua. Lethargic lovers Gremio and Tranio/Lucentio bid to purchase Bianca's hand but dynamic lover Petruchio, aided by his 'best man' Grumio, acts out a comic marriage by capture before the wedding feast can begin. Such behaviour could be taken as a symptom of his 'madness' but more enigmatically Petruchio disrupts the conventional and safe marriage by purchase in order to re-enact an older, more dynamic and in this context a far funnier form of marital behaviour. Petruchio's piratical, militaristic behaviour continues when he 'abducts' Katherine in his deliberate parody of marriage by capture – sweeping through the cramped Paduan society like a philosophical Blackbeard. The language Shakespeare gives him at the end of Act 3, Scene 2 drips with testosterone:

> Touch her whoever dare!
> I'll bring mine action on the proudest he
> That stops my way in Padua. — Grumio,
> Draw forth thy weapon, we are beset with thieves;
> Rescue thy mistress, if thou be a man.
> — Fear not, sweet wench, they shall not touch thee, Kate:
> I'll buckler thee against a million.

The best man

The best man was originally one of the belligerents aiding the bridegroom to carry off the bride in marriage by capture. Its roots are Viking. Behind the high altar of the ancient church at Husaby, Sweden, is a collection of long lances, with sockets for torches. Tradition claims they were given to the groomsmen, the 'best men', as weapons, as well as for illumination, when Scandinavian marriages were solemnised by night. The name 'Grumio', which is reminiscent of groomsman, could be symbolic of the role the character plays in Petruchio's courtship. In medieval times the 'best man' needed to be prepared to shed his blood, if necessary, for his best friend the bridegroom. In the play Grumio comically but loyally draws his weapon when Petruchio asks him.

The bridegroom

The name 'bridegroom' was given to the new husband because custom required him to serve his bride a meal on his wedding day. 'Groom' signified a servant and the 'bride-groom' served the bride. Petruchio serves Katherine food which he has prepared himself in Act 4, Scene 3. When she does not give the customary 'thanks' for such 'kindness', the food is removed and eaten by Hortensio – another disruption of the tradition deliberately orchestrated by Petruchio.

Carrying the bride over the threshold

The custom of carrying the bride over the threshold is a relic of marriage by capture when the woman would be symbolically installed in her new home. Stage directions ('*Enter Petruchio and Katherine*') do not help us when it comes to whether Petruchio carries Katherine over the threshold in Act 4, Scene 1 but directors who understand that Petruchio is re-enacting the customs of marriage by capture will include it – and perhaps add an unceremonious dropping of Katherine when he starts to regale the servants.

Fine clothes

Fine clothes are expected at weddings, symbolically to show the wealth of the participants; the groom's clothes in particular reflect his social standing and capacity to keep his new bride in secure financial circumstances. Though Petruchio tells Baptista and Katherine he will go to Venice to purchase 'fine array' in Act 2, Scene 1 he arrives at his wedding in Act 3, Scene 2 on a diseased, unfit horse, inappropriately dressed in vile old clothes. He refuses several requests to borrow better clothes for the wedding, archly observing: 'To me she's married, not unto my clothes' using his comic disruption to make a serious point. Again the Elizabethan wedding ceremony is important in that it contains an exhortation to wives not to be concerned with 'braided hair, and trimming about with gold, (or) in putting on of gorgeous apparel' as such concern with fripperies will remove the couple's focus on 'mild and quiet' spirituality, 'which is a precious thing in the sight of God'.

In Anglo-Saxon times, the bridegroom tapped his new wife's neck with a shoe which was then placed on the pillow on his side of the bridal bed. If the bride was strong-willed or dominant, a common joke was to move the shoe to the wife's pillow, as a warning to the bridegroom of what he could expect. Petruchio deliberately flings pillows, bolsters and coverlets around the marriage bed to disorientate Katherine. In the Scottish Highlands some wedding guests gently strike either the bride or the bridegroom with an old shoe for luck; in some parts of England, too, the flinging of the shoe or attaching shoes to the back of the honeymoon car is said to be a mode of chastising the bridegroom for taking away the bride; in other words, a survival of claiming a wife by capture. All such customs seem to have their common origin in the shoe anciently received by the bridegroom with the bride. In the final scene, Katherine submits to Petruchio's 'honest will' by symbolically offering to place her hand under his foot, no doubt shod. It is important to notice that Petruchio does not want his wife to perform this symbolic act; instead he asks for a kiss which has its own symbolic meaning of breathing new life into each other. By Act 5, Scene 2 Katherine's and Petruchio's spiritual union is complete.

Taking it further ▶▶

Until recently, corporal punishment showing children being hit with footwear was seen as humorous in British comics featuring such characters as naughty boy Dennis the Menace and naughty girl Minnie the Minx. See http://flickrhivemind.net/User/britishcomicspanking/Recent. What do such images of 'comic' violence tell us about the value systems of British society?

Petruchio is well aware that the conventions of Paduan weddings revolve around the axis of money, making them *de facto* marriages by purchase. He himself says that he is interested in money – which Elizabethan would not be? – but that Shakespeare presents him as going to such lengths to replicate and re-enact the customs and behaviour of marriage by capture signifies that at least part of his nature is anti-establishment. His behaviour before, during and just after the wedding can be described as anarchic.

Working with the text

Assessment Objectives and skills

The examination of English Literature at AS and Advanced Level will test students against five assessment objectives known as AOs. They are:

A01	Articulate informed, personal and creative responses to literary texts, using associated concepts and terminology, and coherent, accurate written expression.
A02	Analyse ways in which meanings are shaped in literary texts.
A03	Demonstrate understanding of the significance and influence of the contexts in which literary texts are written and received.
A04	Explore connections across literary texts.
A05	Explore literary texts informed by different interpretations.

A key feature of A-level and university English Literature is **historicism**: students need to be very familiar with specific social and historical contexts. It is vital for AO3 but also feeds into AOs 4 and 5. Working from the belief that no text exists in isolation but is the product of the time in which it was produced, English Literature encourages students to explore the relationships that exist between texts and the contexts within which they are written, received and understood. The best students debate and challenge the interpretations of critics as they develop their own informed personal responses, analysing the ways in which authors shape meanings. Historicism as it applies to *The Taming of the Shrew* involves thinking about the production of the text at the time of its writing, how the text has been received over time, and exploring how the text can be interpreted now. Texts and their meanings are not fixed, therefore interpretation is not fixed, and multiple interpretations are possible.

Building skills 1: Structuring your writing

This 'Building skills' section focuses upon organising your written responses to convey your ideas as clearly and effectively as possible: the 'how' of your writing as opposed to the 'what'. More often than not, if your knowledge and understanding of *The Taming of the Shrew* is sound, a disappointing mark or grade will be down to one of two common mistakes: misreading the question or failing to organise your response economically and effectively. In an examination you'll be lucky if you can demonstrate 5 per cent of what you know about *Shrew*; luckily, if it's the right 5 per cent, that's all you need to gain full marks.

Understanding your examination

It's important to prepare for the specific type of response your examination body sets with regard to *The Taming of the Shrew*. You'll almost certainly know whether you are studying the play as part of a non-examined assessment unit (i.e. for coursework) or as an examination set text – but you also need to know if your paper is **open book** – i.e. you will have a clean copy of the text available to you in the exam, or **closed book**, in which case you won't. The format of your assessment has major implications for the way you organise your response and dictates the depth and detail required to achieve a top band mark.

Open book

In an open book exam when you have a copy of *Shrew* on the desk in front of you, there can be no possible excuse for failing to quote relevantly, accurately and extensively. To gain a high mark, you are expected to focus in detail on specific passages. Remember, too, that you must not refer to any supporting material such as the Introductory Notes contained within the set edition of your text. If an examiner suspects that you have been lifting chunks of unacknowledged material from such a source, she will refer your paper to the examining body for possible plagiarism.

Closed book

In a closed book exam, because the examiner is well aware that you do not have your text in front of you, their expectations will be different. While you are still expected to support your argument with relevant quotations, close textual references are also rewarded. Since you will have had to memorise quotations, slight inaccuracies will not be severely punished.

Non-examined assessment (NEA)

Writing about *Shrew* within a non-examined assessment (coursework) context poses a very different set of challenges from an examination in that incorrect quotations and disorientating arguments are liable to cost you much more dearly. Your essay must be wholly and consistently relevant to the title selected; there's no excuse for going off track if you or your teacher mapped out the parameters of your chosen topic in the first place.

Step 1: Planning and beginning: Locate the debate

A very common type of exam question invites you to open up a debate about the text by using various trigger words and phrases such as 'consider the view that …', 'some readers think that …' or 'how far do you agree with this view?' When analysing this type of question, you can be certain that exam questions never offer a view that makes no sense whatsoever or a view so blindingly obvious all anyone can do with it is agree; there will always be a genuine interpretation at stake.

Similarly many NEA tasks are written to include a stated view to help give some shape to your writing, so logically your introduction needs to address the terms of this debate and sketch out the outlines of how you intend to move the argument forward to orientate the reader. Therefore, you must plan before you begin to write.

Undertaking a lively debate about some of the ways in which *Shrew* has been and can be interpreted is the DNA of your essay. Any good literary argument needs to be honest but to begin by writing 'Yes, I totally agree with this obviously true statement' suggests a fundamental misunderstanding of what studying literature is all about. Any stated view in an examination question is designed to open up critical conversations, not shut them down.

Plan your answer by collecting together points for and against the given view. Aim to see a stated opinion as an interesting way of focusing upon a key facet of *The Taming of the Shrew*, like the following student.

Student A

This is an A level question of the sort that may be asked on the Edexcel specification.

Explore how Shakespeare uses ideas about female free will in *The Taming of the Shrew*. You must relate your discussion to relevant contextual factors and ideas from your critical reading.

In 'The Taming of The Shrew' the question is not if Katherina undergoes a transformation, but rather is the transformation a consequence of her own free will or a consequence of Petruchio's influence? At the beginning of the play Katherina is a product of her environment; feisty, effervescent but – in my opinion – unhappy. Forced into a marriage market, forced to be a compliant daughter and in constant competition with her sister Bianca, it is debatable that Katherina's nature in the first acts of the play is completely her own, but a consequence of the era, her family and the mercantile environment in which she lives. It can be argued that Petruchio simply gives Kate back to herself. He acknowledges very early on in the play in Act 2, Scene 1 that 'if she be curst it is for policy'. So the 'taming' may be an act of kindness. Yet it is surely beyond all reasonable doubt that Kate has no real say in the matter of her 'taming'. Petruchio says he will tame her 'will you or nill you' so the transformation is not down to her own free will but his. In this regard she is as much a victim of Petruchio's will as Sly was of the lord's moralistic experiment with his identity. Petruchio seems to wear her down with the weight of his speeches. Though Katherine speaks up for herself and answers back, the playwright just does not give her as many lines as he gives to Petruchio. She is trying to communicate her free will by rejecting his odd and completely unexpected proposal 'Let him that moved you hither / Remove you hence' but his energy to bluster his way through seems stronger than hers. Several feminist critics see the Katherina of Act 1 as exhibiting her true nature, before she has been 'tampered with' and made to fit comfortably into her society; they view the intervention of Petruchio as a manipulation of Kate's free will. Could her tenacity and shrewish behaviour be because she has been thrust into a marriage market and forced to be in opposition with her sister Bianca, who has learned earlier than Kate that she must play an acquiescent game in the Paduan world of controlling men?

Examiner's commentary

This student:

▼ acknowledges in the first sentence that there is a debate about whether Kate's transformation is willed by herself or by Petruchio but later goes on to say that it is surely beyond all reasonable doubt that Kate has no real say in the matter of her 'taming'; this argument could be seen as unclear or even contradictory

▼ utilises coherent, accurate written expression and appropriate concepts and terminology within the response but only makes three direct uses of full lines from the play and uses a one-word quotation ('taming') twice; one of the quotations is slightly inaccurate: in Act 2, Scene 1 Petruchio says 'will you or nill you, I will marry you' and this candidate thinks the quotation is about taming rather than marriage

▼ is aware of some of the major themes of the play and does well to mention Sly and the lord from the Induction; the student also does well to give a signpost via a reference to the 'beginning of the play' and demonstrate an understanding of structure but she does not mention the end of the play in this part of the answer

▼ mentions feminist critique but does not make use of specific feminist critics

▼ puts speech marks around phrases which are not contained within *The Taming of the Shrew*, i.e. 'tampered with'

▼ repeats the points that Kate has been thrust into the marriage market and into competition with Bianca; a more sophisticated candidate would perhaps know that she is not in competition with Bianca as Bianca's suitors are not interested in Katherine, nor she them and Baptista has removed any element of genuine competition by stipulating that Katherine must be married before Bianca can be considered for marriage.

In general terms if the rest of her essay reached this level of performance, it is likely she would be on course to achieve a mark of notional grade C.

Instead of using modern adjectives such as 'feisty', 'effervescent' and 'unhappy' the student would have done better if she had used Shakespeare's characters' adjectives such as 'froward', 'mad', 'loud', 'rotten', 'shrewd', 'peevish', 'angry', 'rough' or 'scolding' … there are plenty to choose from. The repetitions also indicate that more careful planning was needed. The ending of the play has been ignored and this is probably an oversight in an analysis of the role of free will in Katherine's journey through the play.

Step 2: Developing and linking: Go with the flow

An essay is a very specific type of formal writing that requires an appropriate discourse structure. In the main body of your writing, you need to thread your developing argument through each paragraph consistently and logically, referring back to the terms established by the question itself, rephrasing and reframing as you go. It can be challenging to sustain the flow of your essay and keep firmly on track, but here are some techniques to help you:

- Ensure your essay doesn't disintegrate into a series of disconnected building blocks by creating a neat and stable bridge between one paragraph and the next.
- Use discourse markers – linking words and phrases like 'on the other hand', 'however', 'although' and 'moreover' – to hold the individual paragraphs of your essay together and signpost the connections between different sections of your overarching argument.
- Having set out an idea in Paragraph A, in Paragraph B you might need to then support it by providing a further example; if so, signal this to the reader with a phrase such as '**Moreover** this imagery of taming a falcon can also be seen when …'
- To change direction and challenge an idea begun in Paragraph A by acknowledging that it is open to interpretation, you could begin Paragraph B with something like '**On the other hand**, this view of the play is challenged by feminist critic Marilyn French …'
- Another typical paragraph-to-paragraph link is when you want to show that the original idea doesn't give the full picture. Here you could modify your original point with something like '**Although** it is entirely possible to view Petruchio's treatment of Katherina as unnecessarily cruel and sexist, this view does not take account of the social context of marriage in the 1590s, when his behaviour may have seemed much less offensive.'

Student B

This is an A-level question of the sort that may be asked on AQA Specification A.

'Katherine remains spirited from the beginning to the end of the play.' In the light of this view, explore how Shakespeare presents Katherine in this extract and elsewhere in the play.

NB The extract is Katherina's speech from Act 5, Scene 2 which begins 'Fie, fie, unknit that threatening unkind brow' and concludes at the end of the play.

In contrast to the early manifestations of Katherine when she was 'curst' and 'froward', her final speech in Act 5, Scene 2 perhaps can be analysed as presenting her as an obedient but realistic wife, rather than the exaggerated 'devil' of Hortensio's and Gremio's imaginings in Act 1, Scene 1. The stage direction 'She obeys' presents a meeker Katherine to the audience than we have been used to, and the fact that she doesn't speak until Petruchio tells her to, adds to the idea that she is now perhaps the model of submissive and dutiful Elizabethan wifehood. However, I disagree with the feminist critique offered by Lise Pederson who argues 'Petruchio consistently plays the role of a bully in his relationship with Kate, and it is, indeed, the means by which he transforms her from a quarrelsome shrew to a sweet-tempered and obedient wife.' Pederson is surely missing the point that on stage there is something rather joyous and gleeful going on between Katherine and Petruchio concerning the 'cap', a real piece of clothing but also an important symbol first seen by Petruchio in Act 4, Scene 3 as a 'lewd and filthy walnut shell' but desired by Katherine as an adornment that 'doth fit the time'. Petruchio isn't a bully in this scene; he is a man of wisdom and humour entirely in keeping with the spirit of the Renaissance. Katherine isn't the unhappy, isolated female she was in Act 1 who mistakenly believed her father was prostituting her by making her a 'stale' for her unprepossessing and pathetic neighbours; she is a confident woman who has found a place in her society and a vibrant new role as a bourgeois and sophisticated wife. The fashionable cap is attractive but it is not important so when Petruchio tells her to 'throw it underfoot' she obeys because the new Katherine, far from having lost her own spirit, now shares her husband's spirited sense of humour and eccentric world view. The gesture reinforces the important point made about marriage in Act 3, Scene 2: 'To me she's married, not unto my clothes.'

Examiner's commentary

This student:

- ↘ expresses her ideas with flair and imagination
- ↘ is comfortable when disagreeing with a very well-known Shakespeare scholar
- ↘ always views the play as a living theatrical experience
- ↘ gracefully shows her understanding of the symbolism of the cap
- ↘ uses signposts to steer her route through the play: Act 5, Scene 2; Act 1, Scene 1; Act 3, Scene 2; and Act 4, Scene 3 are all utilised to great effect
- ↘ uses direct textual evidence as cohesive, coherent staging posts in a well-constructed argument
- ↘ contextualises Elizabethan values and the Renaissance seamlessly
- ↘ is clearly fully engaged with the ideas' networks of T*he Taming of the Shrew.*

If the rest of her essay reached this level of performance, it is likely she would be on course to achieve a notional grade A and is good enough for a notional A*.

Student C

This is a type of A-level question that may be asked on AQA Specification B. This specification requires students to study the play through the lens of comedy.

Read the extract below and then answer the question.

Explore the significance of this extract in relation to the comedy of the play as a whole.

Remember to include in your answer relevant analysis of Shakespeare's dramatic methods.

NB The passage is from Act 3, Scene 2, from Baptista's line 'Is't possible you will away tonight?' (line 187 in most editions) to Petruchio's line 'I'll buckler thee against a million' (line 237 in most editions).

At the beginning of the extract it would appear that Petruchio loves Katherina because he says that he has 'given away' himself to a 'most patient, sweet and virtuous wife' presenting him as a new husband who is very much in love with his new bride. A husband giving himself away instead of a father giving a daughter away could be construed as funny. The phrase shows us that Petruchio has some effeminate qualities. It also shows the reader that he sees himself and Katherina as equals in the sense that they are both giving themselves away to each other. The words 'patient', 'sweet' and 'virtuous' also represent Petruchio's view of Katherine's real nature not tainted by the insults her neighbours and family through at her. There is comedy in this conflict of ideas. Quite soon after this we see the comedy of mockery when it looks as though Petruchio is mocking Katherine when she says 'if you love me, stay' and he replies with 'Grumio, my horse'. This is a comical line that will make the audience laugh because it's suggesting that he doesn't love her at all and doesn't care about her wishes or her happiness. Petruchio just wanted to marry Katherine for money. If Katherine loved him she would want to please him. She even tries to boss around the wedding guests when she says, 'Gentlemen, forward to the bridal dinner' but Petruchio's next announcement is confusing: 'They shall go forward, Kate, at thy command. Obey the bride' which makes it look as though he cares about her a great deal and that she is to be obeyed – the opposite of what she has just promised in church, i.e. she should obey him. Petruchio gets dramatic and potentially violent when he says, 'be mad and merry, or go hang yourselves', which suggests that he cannot truly care about her: what caring husband would tell his new bride's guests to hang themselves? Then he suddenly says 'But for my bonny Kate, she must with me', which must be annoying for Katherina because Petruchio makes it look as if he is on her side and then he contradicts it and takes it all away from her. This is comic. Petruchio claims Katherine as 'his own' and says he will be her 'master'. This is sexist because it shows that he presumes ownership of her and the word 'master' makes it sound like he is going to train her like an animal. This is backed up when he lists off the things that she is for example his 'horse' and his 'ox' but when he says he now owns her 'ass' it shows Petruchio as a sexist. Yet during all of this sexist language he still calls her 'sweet wench' and tells her to 'fear not' which presents in my opinion that Petruchio is playing mind games with his new wife – amusing for the reader but not for Katherine. He confuses her with a combination of love and what can look like cruelty. Which is what he does when he gets her home and the comedy continues.

Examiner's commentary

This student:

- makes a few AO1 errors: 'through' for 'throw' and having variant spellings of Katherine's name (Katherina and Katherine are both acceptable but students need to be consistent); the student also ends on a hanging phrase rather than a full sentence; 'boss around' is a little infelicitous, as is, perhaps, 'mind games'

- attempts to write about comedy and understands that comedy revolves around conflict but is not quite so assured in the section on mockery; there is also a sense that the student, knowing she must write about comedy, lists events in the extract and claims they are comic, sometimes without differentiation

- makes one unintentionally amusing misread when she claims that now they are married Petruchio owns Katherine's 'ass'; the claim that Petruchio is effeminate is perhaps stretching the notion of the examiner 'going with' the student a little too far – Petruchio is one of the most masculine heroes in all of Shakespeare

- does show a competent level of awareness: Petruchio's language veers from the loving to the sexist; Katherine has been misrepresented by the Paduans and might really be sweet, patient and virtuous; this could be funny

- understands some historicity and finds interesting things to say about obedience within Tudor weddings but doesn't fully appreciate the play as a coherent dramatic performance

- sees Petruchio's behaviour as deliberately peculiar and confusing and acknowledges it is funny for the 'reader' (a pity she didn't write about audience) but not for Katherine.

Overall this work would be very near to the C/D grade boundary. It spots and analyses some important language and context features but, like much work at C/D, is hesitant with some ideas and occasionally suffers from weak AO1 expression. The candidate understands that the play has an audience and even identifies Shakespeare as the architect of meaning. However, the work also uses the phrase 'reader' twice which is a shame as this is a drama text and candidates need to be in command of genre to get a higher mark.

Step 3: Concluding: Seal the deal

As you bring your writing to a close, you need to capture and clarify your response to the given view and make a relatively swift and elegant exit. Keep your final paragraph short and sweet. Now is not the time to introduce any new points – but equally, don't just reword everything you have already just said either. Neat potential closers include:

- ◥ looping the last paragraph back to something you mentioned in your introduction to suggest that you have now said all there is to say on the subject
- ◥ reflecting on your key points in order to reach a balanced overview
- ◥ ending with a punchy quotation that leaves the reader thinking
- ◥ discussing the contextual implications of the topic you have debated
- ◥ reversing expectations to end on an interesting alternative view
- ◥ stating why you think the main issue, theme or character under discussion is so central to the play
- ◥ mentioning how different audiences over time might have responded to the topic you have been debating.

Building skills 2: Analysing texts in detail

Act 2, Scene 1

When the couple meet face-to-face in line 180 Petruchio uses the name Kate twelve times in six of his lines between 181 and 189, perhaps to undermine her inferior status by using her 'pet' name, perhaps to establish a familiar rapport following Baptista's example who has just referred to her as 'Kate' in line 166, perhaps to test her mettle when she insists on referring to herself as Katherine. It is hugely significant that he uses the possessive 'my' on the phrase my 'super-dainty Kate' thus demonstrating that he already assumes some form of ownership or entitlement. They banter as a sort of verbal foreplay with Petruchio frequently exploiting opportunities for sexual innuendo: following the joke when Petruchio claims that he will depart with his 'tongue in' her 'tail' (perhaps the first oral sex joke on the English stage) Katherine strikes him; Petruchio does not respond in kind but he does threaten her, 'I swear I'll cuff you if you strike again.' This is the fifth example of Katherine's violent nature in this scene:

1   She drags a bound Bianca around the stage by her wrists.
2   She strikes Bianca at least once.
3   She 'flies after her'.
4   She breaks the lute over Hortensio's head.
5   She strikes Petruchio.

Shakespeare's original audience will probably have found such violence shocking: though comic in some ways, its force and frequency is volcanic. Even a modern audience must wonder if this behaviour needs to be 'curbed' and if the person committing such violence can be said to be in control of herself or in any way be happy. Petruchio has witnessed Katherine's violence twice at first hand now but he eschews his usual bombast and verbal fireworks in favour of a rather cold utterance, beginning in line 271 where his language can be interpreted as mechanistically business-like when he says:

Taking it further ▶

Research images of medieval and early modern domestic violence to see what they can add to your understanding of the violence presented in the play.

> Thus in plain terms: your father hath consented
> That you shall be my wife, your dowry 'greed on,
> And will you, nill you, I will marry you.

'Plain' is the only adjective and the verbs 'shall' and 'will' imply a *fait accompli*. Petruchio reinforces Katherine's lack of choice and her father's patriarchal control in the phrases 'your father hath consented' and 'your dowry 'greed on'. The transitive verb phrase 'nill you' underlines Katherine's inability to refuse as Shakespeare gives Petruchio an early modern version of the word '*nihil*', the Latin noun for 'nothing', combining it with '*nyllan*' the Old English verb for 'refuse'. However, just at the point when Petruchio could be interpreted as a domineering, inflexible misogynist, Shakespeare immediately changes the wooer's tack in order to give the audience and Katherine yet another perspective of Petruchio, who now attempts to make Katherine see herself in a different *light*, consciously utilising the word in relation to her beauty:

> For, by this light whereby I see thy beauty —
> Thy beauty that doth make me like thee well —
> Thou must be married to no man but me,
> For I am he born to tame you, Kate.

Do we detect that he is telling the truth? The repetition of the noun 'beauty' echoes the first use of the word in line 191 and his constant sexual punning (in addition to the oral sex joke): 'come sit on me'; 'women are made to bear'; 'a combless cock'; 'warm … in thy bed' has made it very clear that he is sexually attracted to her. Critics such as Maynard Mack in *Engagement and Detachment in Shakespeare's Plays* (Columbia, University of Missouri Press, 1962), who see Katherine as the shrew and Petruchio as her wise therapist, suggest that Petruchio's favourable descriptions of Katherine are part of his therapy, designed to show her the beautiful woman she can become if she modifies her behaviour. However, it can be argued just as validly that Petruchio does not encourage Katherine to see her beauty as a thing of the future but as an aspect of her current life, true of her life in the here and now, despite what Hortensio and Gremio may think.

Petruchio has already introduced fanciful claims about Katherine having a limp, which is clearly not true, so he has set a precedent of telling some truths in the midst of wild exaggeration. If the audience is disorientated, so too is Katherine: Petruchio is the arch disrupter of convention and expectation. He continues to imply a certain fatalism about their relationship, claiming that he 'must' marry Katherine and that he is the man 'born to tame' her which he immediately turns upside down in the phrase 'no man but me', implying that Katherine has a queue of other men also prepared to marry her, when both the audience and Katherine know she is unpopular and isolated in Padua. In this way Shakespeare makes Petruchio suggest that Katherine's life contains some choice despite the overarching fatalism that they are destined to be together. He is essentially presenting himself as the reconciler of what has hitherto been impossible in Katherine's life: she is destined to have a happy life via a fulfilling sexualised marriage but she will, up to a point, choose this path. Petruchio will still be the agent of her fortune, having the power to transform her from a wild Kate into a household Kate. The pun on 'wild Kate' is at least double-edged, carrying the meaning not only of 'wildcat' but also of 'wild kite' (falcon), thus introducing the hawking metaphor which will become such an important part of the play from Act 4 onwards.

This exchange lays out the terms for the couple's later relationship: Petruchio will out-talk Katherine and at times he will dominate her but he will also fascinate her. True, when Baptista reappears, Katherine attacks him for his lack of 'fatherly regard' in consenting to a marriage to a 'madcap ruffian' but Petruchio appears to intrigue her when he tells the assembled Paduans that if Katherine is curst 'it is for policy' which is a highly sensitive analysis of her situation. True again, she says she will see him 'hanged' before she will marry him in line 302 but when Petruchio stifles Gremio's and Tranio's criticism with the lines 'I choose her for myself; / If she and I be pleased, what's that to you?' Katherine remains silent and maintains her silence for 26 lines until the conclusion of the scene. Completely aware of Petruchio's plans for their wedding, by failing to protest further against his false claim that they have reached a private agreement, the audience may consider that Katherine implicitly consents to marry him. Perhaps his claim that he has chosen her for personal reasons — i.e. because of her thrice-praised 'beauty' rather than her once-mentioned dowry — has thrilled and excited her.

Extended commentaries

Petruchio's soliloquy, Act 4, Scene 1

The scene is peppered with references to falconry. Eleven words are taken directly from the manuals of the day: 'sharp' (famished); 'stoop' (to swoop and fly to the lure); 'full-gorged' (allowed to eat her fill); 'lure' (apparatus such as a bunch of feathers or a decoy bird which the falcon would catch in mid-air in order to retrieve and eat the meat attached); 'man' (a verb meaning the process by which a wild bird is trained to become accustomed to, not to be afraid of and to trust men — particularly relevant to Katherine, whose extreme behaviour may indicate her fear of men before Petruchio's intervention); 'haggard' (wild hawk); 'watch' (a verb meaning to keep the hawk awake and watchful); 'kites' (general term for hawks and falcons); 'bate' (grow angry); 'beat' (the flapping of the bird's wings). When the long and exhausting process of manning was complete a close and special bond between man and hawk was established, joining them together as an efficient team. Brian Morris in the Arden edition of 1981 expresses surprise that the hawking motif is introduced so comparatively late in the play but references to falconry have been in the play from the Induction: 'Thou hast hawks will soar / Above the morning lark.' Several references to hawking are used of Bianca: Gremio asks Baptista 'Will you mew her up?' and Tranio when reporting back to Lucentio about how difficult it is to gain access to

Bianca says that her father has 'closely mewed her up'. Petruchio also hints at hawking when he reveals to Katherine that he will bring her from a 'wild Kate' into a Kate 'as conformable as other household Kates', with the pun in the first usage perhaps referring to wild kites as much as wild cats. In Act 3, Scene 1 Hortensio, suspecting Bianca of preferring 'Cambio', describes her as 'ranging', a reference to a hawk straying from her lure, and in Act 4, Scene 2 Hortensio will call Bianca a 'haggard,' a term Shakespeare often uses to communicate wildness in women.

In depriving Katherine of sex on her wedding night Petruchio deprives himself not only of a pleasure but an activity which was the final stage in the process of the achievement of a state of grace.

For a marriage to be viewed as legal and binding in Elizabethan society and in the eyes of the church, three distinct stages were necessary: the first was the reading of the banns; the second was the service; and the third was the consummation of marriage achieved by the partners having sexual intercourse. At this point in the play Petruchio and Katherine have only achieved the first two stages. The audience is left to assume that the consummation does not occur until after the wedding feast in Act 5, Scene 2, that is to say that when Petruchio and Katherine leave the stage to 'go to bed' they will consummate their marriage. Why does Petruchio wait until Act 5, Scene 2 to have sex with his new bride? One suggestion is that until he feels she is happy and settled that to have sex with her would be a form of exploitation, hardly the act of the sadistic rapist presented by Charles Marowitz in his 1975 adaptation *The Shrew*.

Petruchio plans to deprive Katherine of sleep but by doing so he will deprive himself of sleep. There is a sense of mutuality about Petruchio in this scene as elsewhere in the play which can cut through any discomfort felt by the acknowledgement that he is changing Katherine's behaviour by making her adjust to his world of stimulus and reward.

Context

In the Elizabethan reformed church as well as within Roman Catholicism marriage was the only Christian sacrament that people could bestow on themselves; all other sacraments relied on the mediation of a clergyman who acted as a conduit between humankind and the godhead.

Katherine's concluding speech, Act 5, Scene 2

Katherine's speech, the longest she has in the play, lays out the *quid pro quos* of marriage in what is in effect a sermon. Triplets abound on single lines: 'lord', 'king', 'governor / thy lord', 'thy life', 'thy keeper / thy head', 'thy sovereign', 'one that cares for thee', 'warm', 'secure', 'safe / love', 'fair looks', 'true obedience / rule', 'supremacy', 'sway / serve', 'love', 'obey / soft', 'weak', 'smooth'.

Katherine uses other features of lists on single lines too. In addition to the eight triplets, Shakespeare gives Katherine two quartets: 'muddy', 'ill-seeming', 'thick', 'bereft of beauty / froward', 'peevish', 'sullen', 'sour'. The playwright also makes extensive use of words and phrases in pairs on single lines: 'unknit', 'unkind / glances', 'eyes / blots thy beauty', 'bite the meads / confounds fame', 'shake buds / meet', 'amiable / woman moved', 'fountain troubled / dry', 'thirsty / sip', 'touch / thy maintenance', 'his body / sea and land / night in storms', 'day in cold / little payment', 'great a debt / subject', 'prince / woman', 'husband / obedient', 'honest / graceless traitor', 'loving lord / offer war', 'kneel for peace / toil and trouble / soft conditions', 'hearts / froward and unable (worms) / 'word for word', 'frown for frown / lances', 'straws / strength as weak'.

The cumulative effect of the 23 paired iterations, the eight triplets and the two quartets is astonishing: though the language is measured and calm as dictated by the stately iambic pentameter the impact on the listener is akin to being under verbal precision-bombing aimed by a professor of rhetoric. No one interrupts Katherine or talks over or across her. No one ignores her. Everyone listens. For the first time in her life she is centre stage because of the power of her persuasive words, not her violent actions. Her speech which outlines marriage as a contract arranged around a mutual 'debt' takes nouns from the natural world: 'frosts', 'meads', 'whirlwinds', 'buds', 'fountain', 'sea', 'land', 'night', 'storms', 'day', 'worms' and 'straws' to make the male-female relationship seem natural and reasonable. Unreasonable women are described with derogatory adjectives: 'threatening', 'unkind', 'scornful', 'troubled', 'muddy', 'ill-seeming', 'thick', 'dry', 'froward', 'peevish', 'sullen', 'sour', 'foul', 'contending', 'graceless', 'simple' and 'unable'. Women who accept the natural order of things and who understand that 'loving' men care for their wives, undertake 'painful labour' and 'toil and trouble in the world' will be rewarded and Shakespeare gives Katherine a string of adjectives of comfort to exemplify this: 'warm', 'secure', 'safe'. To show that appreciation is warranted for such male duties, Katherine describes a thankful woman's gratitude with the adjectives 'fair' and 'true'. Katherine hints at the sexual rewards of marriage via the erotic adjectives 'soft' (which she repeats) and 'smooth' when she describes the female body. She speaks with enthusiasm about women lying 'warm at home' in an echo of Petruchio's desire to be warm in Katherine's bed.

Of course, on stage, Katherine can say these lines ironically or mechanically as though she does not truly believe them or is mouthing Petruchio's words and not using her own. The speech may be her final defeat and her language which can be seen as exaggerated due to its rhetorical lists and references to war may be considered to be illustrative of a military defeat. However, it is useful to compare the ending of the anonymous *A Shrew* with Shakespeare's ending. In *A Shrew* the Katherine character (Kate) speaks of 'the King of Kings, the glorious God of Heaven' who has ordained the universe and all things in it. This God plucked out Adam's rib and from it made an inferior creature, a woman, who caused man's fall from paradise and was forever after the 'woe of man'; thus Kate offers obedience due to the great crime women committed against men. Shakespeare's Katherine does not adhere to this model of inflexible hierarchical patriarchy steeped in Old Testament superstition but instead offers a new model of companionable, modern marriage based on the Renaissance ideals of mutuality, reason and choice.

Induction, Scene 1:

Lord: O monstrous beast, how like a swine he lies!
Grim death, how foul and loathsome is thine image
Sirs, I will practise on this drunken man.
What think you, if he were coveyed to bed,
Wrapped in sweet clothes, rings put upon his fingers,
A most delicious banquet by his bed,
And brave attendants near him when he wakes,
Would not the beggar then forget himself?

1

> ◀ *Shrew* has many references to food or the lack of it and 'banquet'
> helps establish the idea of nourishment provided and denied.
> However, perhaps the most interesting idea here is that of disguise
> and making things appear to be other than they are. The lord
> is suggesting what can be seen as a rather cruel psychological
> experiment: to persuade Sly that his real identity (a drunken tinker)
> has been but a dream and that he is a powerful aristocrat. That this
> is done for 'jest' is perhaps morally dubious.

Act 1, Scene 1:

Baptista: Gentlemen, importune me no farther,
For how I firmly am resolved you know:
That is, not to bestow my youngest daughter
Before I have a husband for the elder.
If either of you both love Katherina,
Because I know you well and love you well,
Leave shall you have to court her at your pleasure.

2

Gremio: To cart her, rather. She's too rough for me.

> ◀ Shakespeare here establishes the vital plot strand of Bianca having
> to wait until Katherine is married before she can be wed. Katherine
> is clearly unimpressed with the suitors Gremio and Hortensio and
> demonstrates her reluctance to comply with the social convention
> of being courted by people she considers to be foolish and beneath
> her own aspirations. Typically for Katherine early in the play, her
> unhappiness and anger are accompanied by the threat of violence.
> This can be amusing or a little sad, depending upon how the director
> wants to play the scene. Katherine appears either oblivious to the
> fact that neither man wants anything to do with her or is enraged
> by it. Just as the lord viewed Sly as subhuman ('monstrous beast',

'swine'), Hortensio views Katherine as somehow not truly human when he refers to her as a 'devil'. Katherine thinks her father wishes to treat her as a breeding mare or worse ('stale' frequently means prostitute in Elizabethan English) for the amusement and pleasure of his acquaintances ('mates').

3

Act 1, Scene 1:

Tranio: You will be schoolmaster,
And undertake the teaching of the maid:
That's your device.

Lucentio: It is. May it be done?

Tranio: Not possible: for who shall bear your part
And be in Padua here Vincentio's son,
Keep house and ply his book, welcome his friends,
Visit his countrymen and banquet them?

Lucentio: *Basta*, content thee, for I have it full.
Then it follows thus:
Thou shalt be master, Tranio, in my stead.

> Modern Italian uses the word '*suppositi*' as 'exchanged' and here Lucentio and Tranio exchange identities so Lucentio can gain access to Bianca. This plot device of servants exchanging identities with their masters goes back as far as Menander, a Greek playwright active around 320–290 BC. Greek comedy inspired the Roman playwright Terence (195–159 BC) whose *Eunuch* is often cited as an inspiration to Ariosto. Plautus developed the character of the 'clever slave' and here we see Shakespeare give the role of clever servant to Tranio via Plautus' *Mostellaria*: not only has Tranio to be completely convincing in his role of Lucentio the gentleman scholar but also must think and act quickly when unexpected things occur in the plot. Yet again, following the Induction, the notion of the world turned upside down by subterfuge, disguises, exchanged identities, bare-faced lying and playing tricks is placed before the audience. In the theatre this scene can be very amusing as it affords the actors the opportunity to do a quick-change routine.

4

Act 1, Scene 2:

Petruchio: Think you a little din can daunt mine ears?
Have I not in my time heard lions roar?
Have I not heard the sea, puffed up with winds,
Rage like an angry boar chafed with sweat?
Have I not heard great ordnance in the field,
And heaven's artillery thunder in the skies?

Have I not in a pitched battle heard
Loud 'larums, neighing steeds, and trumpets' clang?
And do you tell me of a woman's tongue,
That gives not half so great a blow to hear
As will a chestnut in a farmer's fire?
Tush, tush, fear boys with bugs.

▼ This rousing speech full of militaristic pomp and swagger gives plenty of scope for the director and actor working together: is Petruchio really so much larger than life as this speech suggests or is he a pompous braggart who will be put in his place by the fearsome female? The audience now can't wait for the first meeting between Katherine and Petruchio who are clearly the most vibrant and colourful characters in the play. See the commentary on Act 1, Scene 2 for a fuller explanation.

Act 2, Scene 1:

5

Petruchio:	Come, come, you wasp, i' faith you are too angry.
Katherine:	If I be waspish, best beware my sting.
Petruchio:	My remedy is then to pluck it out.
Katherine:	Ay, if the fool could find it where it lies.
Petruchio:	Who knows not where a wasp does wear his sting? In his tail.
Katherine:	In his tongue.
Petruchio:	Whose tongue?
Katherine:	Yours, if you talk of tales, and so farewell.
Petruchio:	What, with my tongue in your tail? / Nay, come again, good Kate, I am a gentleman—
Katherine:	That I'll try. (*She strikes him*)
Petruchio:	I swear I'll cuff you if you strike again.

▼ This is a very funny and a very revealing exchange; it relies on witty wordplay of a highly sexual nature and Katherine (like other Shakespearean heroines) shows she can give as good as she gets in trading double-entendres. Yet Petruchio's ribald humour provokes a violent reaction. At this point most directors make it obvious that Katherine has met her match: after he has warned her that he will retaliate physically she does not strike again. Many directors make it clear that there is a sexual chemistry at work between Petruchio and Katherine. If *Shrew* were a pure farce Shakespeare could have followed the 'Punch and Judy' route and had Petruchio knock about his wife-to-be. Yet the playwright rejects violence for Petruchio, setting him on a much more subtle psychological course.

6

Act 2, Scene 1:

Katherine: Call you me daughter? Now I promise you
You have showed a tender fatherly regard
To wish me wed to one half lunatic,
A madcap ruffian and a swearing Jack
That thinks with oaths to face the matter out.

Petruchio: Father, 'tis thus: yourself and all the world
That talked of her have talked amiss of her.
If she be curst, it is for policy,
For, she's not froward, but modest as the dove;
She is not hot, but temperate as the morn;
For patience she will prove a second Grissel,
And Roman Lucrece for her chastity;
And to conclude, we have 'greed so well together
That upon Sunday is the wedding-day.

Katherine: I'll see thee hanged on Sunday first.

Gremio: Hark, Petruchio, she says she'll see thee hanged first.

Tranio: Is this your speeding? Nay, then, goodnight our part!

Petruchio: Be patient, gentlemen. I choose her for myself;
If she and I be pleased, what's that to you?

Katherine has been disorientated by the speed and manner of Petruchio's eccentric and unconventional wooing and she vents her spleen on Baptista for matching her with a 'madcap half lunatic'. Petruchio's response is revealing and demonstrates that he has spotted something in her nature which is indicative of both his own intelligence and his growing sympathy for hers: 'If she be curst, it is for policy'. It may seem preposterous to the others – even perhaps to Katherine herself – but her wild behaviour up to now has been a defence mechanism. Petruchio goes further and in only one of many sage observations in *The Taming of the Shrew* about marriage he defends his choice of bride – 'I choose her for myself' – which can be interpreted as Petruchio's confession that he is choosing her for his own reasons, not entirely financial or mercenary. The emphasis on the importance of marriage as an exclusive partnership which should not be subject to the external pressures of family and what friends and acquaintances may think is boldly stated in the question 'If she and I be pleased what's that to you?' For the early 1590s this is a radical, egalitarian and thought-provoking question.

Act 3, Scene 2:

7

Baptista: What will be said? What mockery will it be
              To want the bridegroom when the priest attends
              To speak the ceremonial rites of marriage?
              What says Lucentio to this shame of ours?

Katherine: No shame but mine. I must, forsooth, be forced
              To give my hand opposed against my heart
              Unto a mad-brain rudesby, full of spleen
              Who wooed in haste and means to wed at leisure.
              I told you, I, he was a frantic fool,
              Hiding his bitter jests in blunt behaviour,
              And, to be noted for a merry man,
              He'll woo a thousand, 'point the day of marriage,
              Make feast, invite friends, and proclaim the banns,
              Yet never means to wed where he hath wooed.
              Now must the world point at poor Katherine
              And say, 'Lo, there is mad Petruccio's wife,
              If it would please him come and marry her!'

Petruchio has decided to keep up his madman act by not turning up on time for his wedding and when he does arrive shortly after this extract he is wearing such bizarre clothes that the opportunity for visual comedy is at its highest. Petruchio uses the general consternation about him not wearing the appropriate conventional apparel to make a splendid point about the vacuousness of fashion versus the seriousness of marriage: 'To me she's married, not unto my clothes'. Yet despite the colourful eccentricities of wardrobe and behaviour and the many opportunities for rollicking farce, in this scene Katherine's sense of disappointment and hurt are palpable. She still claims she is giving her hand without her heart and she seems genuinely fearful that Petruchio is genuinely unhinged and that she will be scoffed and pointed out as a madman's wife. More than this, however, lies the possibility that she cannot bear the thought of being stood up on her wedding day. Her vulnerability is all the more affecting because, even though we are now well into Act 3, it is the first time that Shakespeare has shown Katherine's softer nature to the audience.

Act 4, Scene 1:

8

Petruchio: My falcon now is sharp and passing empty,
              And till she stoop she must not be full-gorged,
              For then she never looks upon her lure.
              Another way I have to man my haggard,
              To make her come, and know her keeper's call:

That is, to watch her, as we watch these kites
That bate, and beat, and will not be obedient.
She ate no meat today, nor none shall eat;
Last night she slept not, nor tonight she shall not;
As with the meat, some undeserved fault
I'll find about the making of the bed,
And here I'll fling the pillow, there the bolster,
This way the coverlet, another way the sheets.
Ay, and amid this hurly I intend
That all is done in reverend care of her.

Sleep deprivation and starvation are now rightly judged as torture and much has been made of this speech in which Petruchio in soliloquy outlines his plans to 'tame a shrew' in the manner that a falconer would train a wild bird. Many observers find Petruchio's references to Katherine as an animal ('falcon', 'kite') and to her bating, beating disobedience, which must be prevented, as extremely distasteful. Erin Furstnau in her article 'Feminist Themes in and Critiques of Shakespeare's *Taming of the Shrew*' claims there is 'an awkward seriousness in Petruchio's treatment of Katherine that borders on something darkly misogynistic rather than comedic.' Other voices argue that we should not take a farce too seriously or that the whole play including the Induction is a satire against misogynistic patriarchy. For other scholars the play shows Petruchio mirroring Katherine's own early extreme behaviour so that she may better understand herself and change. When this author directed the play in the USA that is the stance he took. Theatre productions and films can help students arrive at their own understanding. Does Petruchio starve himself as well as Katherine? He certainly denies himself sex on his wedding night. How does the actor express the line 'That all is done in reverend care of her'?

9 Act 5, Scene 1:

Lucentio: Love wrought these miracles. Bianca's love
Made me exchange my state with Tranio
While he did bear my countenance in the town,
And happily I have arrived at the last
Unto the wished haven of my bliss.
What Tranio did, myself enforced him to;
Then pardon him, sweet father, for my sake.

Vincentio: I'll slit the villain's nose that would have sent me to the jail.

Baptista: But do you hear, sir? Have you married my daughter without asking my good will?

Vincentio: Fear not, Baptista, we will content you—go to. But I will in to be revenged for this villainy.

                                                                 Exit

Baptista:	And I to sound the depth of this knavery.	*Exit*
Lucentio:	Look not pale, Bianca, thy father will not frown.	
	Exeunt (Lucentio and Bianca)	
Gremio:	My cake is dough, but I'll in among the rest, Out of hope of all but my share of the feast.	*Exit*
Katherine:	Husband, let's follow to see the end of this ado.	
Petruchio:	First kiss me, Kate, and we will.	

In this scene the various disguises and exchanged personalities are unravelled. Despite Lucentio's confidence to Bianca ('thy father will not frown'), Vincentio is still very aggrieved, threatening some nose-slitting as 'revenge' for the villainy he has suffered and Baptista is unhappy about the 'knavery' of Lucentio secretly marrying Bianca without his 'good will' or blessing. Part of the comic tradition is for the young people to trick or outwit the older generation. Grumio sees the planned subterfuges and disguises in this way when in Act 1, Scene 2 he says 'See, to beguile the old folks, how the young folks lay their heads together' yet despite the expectation of chicanery the audience may feel a little uncomfortable that Lucentio still has some wheedling to perform before he gets out of the scrape he is in with his father and Baptista. The now open and apparently happy relationship which exists between Katherine and Petruchio is offered as a contrast to Lucentio's and Bianca's marriage of stealth. Petruchio can ask his wife for a kiss in the street and she can comply only fearing for her 'modesty' which was once the sole prevail of her sister.

Act 5, Scene 2:

10

Katherine:	Thy husband is thy lord, thy life, thy keeper, Thy head, thy sovereign: one that cares for thee And for thy maintenance; commits his body To painful labour both by sea and land, [...] Such duty as the subject owes the prince, Even such a woman oweth to her husband; And when she is froward, peevish, sullen, sour, And not obedient to his honest will, What is she but a foul contending rebel And graceless traitor to her loving lord? I am ashamed that women are so simple To offer war where they should kneel for peace, Or seek for rule, supremacy, and sway When they are bound to serve, love, and obey.

This 'obedience speech' is the most controversial in the play and the successful student needs to do at least two things with it: to examine it from the perspective of the play's original audience and to examine it from a modern viewpoint. The majority of the original audience would have probably held the view that the world and beyond that creation itself comprised a hierarchy and a series of God-ordained interrelationships. Thus there were nine ranks of angels, the highest of which were closest to God.

Creation was a 'Chain of Being' where women were placed a little lower than men. Katherine acknowledges this: 'Thy husband is thy lord, thy life, thy keeper, / Thy head, thy sovereign' and goes on to talk about the happiness that will accrue in accepting this arrangement: while your husband commits to painful labour and dangerous occupations you can lie 'warm at home, secure and safe'. However, within this arrangement it is imperative that the husband does not assume that he has tyrannical powers. Katherine makes it clear that the wife is only bound to be obedient to her husband's *honest* will. Shakespeare is careful to make Katherine echo the words of the marriage service from the Book of Common Prayer in which the woman must promise to obey, serve, love, honour and keep her husband in sickness and in health. Katherine's speech then is a defence of the typical Elizabethan happy marriage. Problems for today's audiences revolve around the fact that most of us no longer believe that a wife is inferior 'in degree' to her husband and in this regard the whole speech can be seen as degrading and upsetting. However, at the end of the play Katherine and Petruchio seem destined for a happier marriage than Lucentio and Bianca and Hortensio and the widow.

Context

The Nine Ranks of Angels

The Dionysius who wrote *On the Celestial Hierarchy* (fourth or fifth century) and Thomas Aquinas (*Summa Theologica*, circa 1270) utilised the New Testament, specifically Ephesians 1:21 and Colossians 1:16, to promote the notion of three Hierarchies of angels, with each Hierarchy containing three Orders (Ranks) or Choirs. In the first Choir closest to God are Seraphim, Cherubim and Thrones. In the middle Choir are Dominions, Virtues and Powers and in the third Choir closest to humankind are Archangels, Principalities and Angels.

Books

- Bates, Alfred (ed.), *The Drama: Its History, Literature and Influence on Civilization*, Vol. 1, London: Historical Publishing Company, 1906.
  - Bates presents a fascinating early-twentieth-century account of the importance and impact of Drama on Civilization from its beginnings. Volume 1 deals with Greek Drama.
- French, Marilyn, *Shakespeare's Division of Experience*, New York: Ballantine, 1981.
  - French offers a fairly straightforward feminist analysis of Shakespeare's plays based on the premise that certain characteristics of human behaviour have been characterised as feminine or masculine.
- Hodgdon, Barbara, Introduction to the Arden Shakespeare edition of *The Taming of the Shrew*, Bloomsbury: Arden, 2010.
  - This is an effective and scholarly introduction to the play.
- Holderness, Graham, *The Taming of the Shrew*, Manchester: Manchester University Press, 1989.
  - Holderness presents a résumé of textual criticism – especially Marxism and feminism – and examines historical stagings in conjunction with such modern productions such as the RSC versions of John Barton in 1960 and Michael Bogdanov in 1978, Franco Zeffirelli's 1966 film and Jonathan Miller's 1982 BBC production.
- Masefield, John, *William Shakespeare*, New York: Henry Holt, 1911.
  - This book is an example of the sort of biography popular before the development of modern critical theory: as such, to modern eyes it lacks direction and purpose claiming that because Masefield did not like, for example, *Measure for Measure* or *All's Well That Ends Well* they were 'second-rank' plays.
- Ornstein, Robert, *Shakespeare's Comedies*, Newark: University of Delaware Press, 1986.
  - In this award-winning book Ornstein argues that critical attempts to reduce the comedies to a single formula are unsatisfactory. Of particular interest is his opinion that though early comedies are festive in nature, they contain notes of sadness not present in his source materials.
- Richmond, Hugh M., *Shakespeare's Sexual Comedy: A Mirror for Lovers*, New York: Bobbs-Merrill, 1971.
  - Richmond argues that Petruchio's 'taming' of Katherine does not break her spirit but teaches her a 'more effective social stance' so that she is

actually more powerful by the end of the play and is more 'dominant' than she has ever been.

▼ Strong, Roy, *The Cult of Elizabeth; Elizabethan Portraiture and Pageantry*, London: Pimlico, 1999.

  — Strong examines the symbolic importance of portrait painting with particular concentration on Queen Elizabeth I.

▼ Van Doren, Mark, *Shakespeare*, New York: Henry Holt, 1939.

  — This is a useful play-by-play analysis of Shakespeare's work in what Van Doren considers to be their chronological order. Based on the author's Shakespeare lectures at Columbia University, which paid attention to character, language and mood, it is a good companion to Harold Bloom's *Shakespeare: the Invention of the Human* to see what two giants of American scholarship, one in 1939; the other in 1998 think of the canon.

▼ Wilson, Edwin (ed.), *Shaw on* Shakespeare, London: Cassell, 1961.

  — Witty and provocative, Shaw's dislike for Shakespeare is collated from across his writing and presented here by Wilson. Shaw claimed 'With the single exception of Homer, there is no eminent writer, not even Sir Walter Scott, whom I can despise so entirely as I despise Shakespeare when I measure my mind against his'. Of the conclusion of *The Taming of the Shrew* Shaw claimed 'No man with any decency of feeling can sit out (the final act) in the company of a woman without being extremely ashamed.'

Articles and essays

▼ Bergeron, David M., 'The Wife of Bath and Shakespeare's *The Taming of the Shrew*', *University Review* 35, 1969.

  — Bergeron analyses links between Chaucer's and Shakespeare's presentations of spirited women.

▼ Brooks, Charles, 'Shakespeare's Romantic Shrews', *Shakespeare Quarterly* 11, 1960.

  — This is an interesting comparison of Katherine in *The Taming of the Shrew* and Adriana in *The Comedy of Errors*.

▼ Brown, Carolyn E., 'Bianca and Petruchio: "The Veriest Shrew[s] of All"' *Re-Visions of Shakespeare: Essays in Honor of Robert Ornstein*, Evelyn Gajowski (ed.), Newark, DE: University of Delaware Press, 2004.

  — Brown argues that among Shakespeare's 'shrews' there is something unsettling and unusual about the presentation of Katherine because it is so 'different from the rest of the comedies in which Shakespeare shows appreciation for the woman's situation'.

▼ Clark, Sandra, 'The Taming of the Shrew and Popular Culture', Shakespeare Newsletter, Spring 2003.
  – Clark argues that Shakespeare was tapping into the popular culture of his own time to create the play.

▼ Coghill, Nevill, 'The Basis of Shakespearian Comedy', Shakespeare Criticism, 1935–60, Anne Ridler (ed.), London: Oxford University Press, 1963.
  – Coghill places The Taming of the Shrew and other Shakespeare comedies within the mediaeval tradition of improvement in which the plot moves from a sad beginning to a happy ending rather than within the Renaissance tradition of ridicule.

▼ Costa, Maddy, 'The Taming of the Shrew: This is not a woman being crushed' (www.theguardian.com/stage/2012/jan/17/taming-of-the-shrew-rsc)
  – This is an interesting article about different interpretations of the Katherine–Petruchio relationship from recent productions.

▼ Fay, E.W., 'Further Notes on the Mostellaria of Plautus', The American Journal of Philology, Vol. 24, No. 3, John Hopkins University Press, 1903.
  – Though dated, this is a good source for anyone interested in Plautus' Mostellaria.

▼ Fineman, Joel, 'The Turn of the Shrew', Shakespeare and the Question of Theory, Patricia Parker and Geoffrey Hartman (eds), New York: Methuen, 1985.
  – Fineman argues that the Shakespearean age invented a new model of human personality which informed the composition of Shakespeare's sonnets and plays. Fineman's work is eclectic but is essentially motivated by Lacanian psychoanalysis.

▼ Furstnau, Erin, 'Feminist Themes in and Critiques of Shakespeare's Taming of the Shrew', www2.cedarcrest.edu/academic/eng/lfletcher/shrew/efurstnau.htm
  – This is another feminist reading of the play which casts Petruchio as 'darkly misogynistic.'

▼ Hartwig, Joan, 'Horses and Women in The Taming of the Shrew', Huntington Library Quarterly 45, 1982.
  – Feminist Hartwig argues that Petruchio views Katherine as a horse and that his method of taming her equates to the Elizabethan manner of taming a horse. She illustrates her article with plates showing scolds' bridles and other instruments of torture despite their clear non-appearance in the play at any point.

▼ Hazlitt, William, 'On Wit and Humour' in English Comic Writers, 1819.
  – A humane and entertaining analysis of comedy: 'Man is the only animal that laughs and weeps; for he is the only animal that is struck with the difference between what things are, and what they ought to be.'

▼ Heilman, Robert, 'The Taming Untamed; or The Return of the Shrew', *Modern Language Quarterly* 27, 1966.

– Heilman attempts to cut through the criticism that psychoanalyses the protagonists or views them only through modern eyes, by calling for the play to be re-evaluated as a farce.

▼ Hibbard, George R., '*The Taming of the Shrew*: A Social Comedy', *Shakespearean Essays*, Alwin Thaler and Norman Sanders (eds), Knoxville: University of Tennessee Press, 1964.

– Hibbard argues that underneath the rollicking comedy the play 'portrays the marriage situation … as it was in Shakespeare's England. The play's disapproval of the arranged match, in which no account is taken of the feelings of the principals, could not be plainer. Within the framework of marriage as it existed at the time, it comes out in favour of the match based on real knowledge and experience'. Hibbard's sentiments are not generally popular with feminists.

▼ Hodgdon, Barbara, 'Katherina Bound; or, Play(K)ating the Strictures of Everyday Life', *PMLA* 107, No. 3, 1992.

– Hodgdon uses new feminism, Marxism and historicism to investigate the gender politics of the play's Elizabethan contexts as well as those of twentieth-century film and video reproductions to find that lurking behind the facades of farce and romantic comedy the play explores sado-masochism and makes new patriarchies and new myths about women.

▼ Hunt, Maurice, 'Homeopathy in Shakespearean Comedy and Romance', *Ball State University Forum* 29, 1988.

– Hunt views Petruchio as a type of doctor skilled in homeopathic therapies with Katherine as his 'patient'. Petruchio's intervention helps Katherine 'achieve a truer self, one freed, for instance, from … the trap of shrewishness'.

▼ Huston, J. Dennis, '"To Make a Puppet": Play and Play-Making in *The Taming of the Shrew*', *Shakespeare Studies* 9, 1976.

– This article presents Petruchio as rebelling against the conventions of classic Greek New Comedy. Though elements of New Comedy are present in *The Taming of the Shrew* (a tight plot and recurring stock characters such as the cunning slave or servant) Petruchio is essentially an unconventional hero.

▼ Kahn, Coppelia, '*The Taming of the Shrew*: Shakespeare's Mirror of Marriage' in *The Authority of Experience: Essays in Feminist Criticism*, Arlyn Diamond and Lee R.. Edwards (eds), Amherst: University of Massachusetts Press, 1977.

– Kahn offers a conventional feminist critique of the play.

▼ Miller, Stephen, 'The Taming of a Shrew and the Theories or Though This Be Badness, yet There Is Method in't', *Textual Formations and Reformations*, Laurie E. Maguire and Thomas L. Berger (eds), Newark, DE: University of Delaware Press, 1998.

  — Miller offers a careful examination of the links between *The Taming of a Shrew* published 1594 and Shakespeare's *The Taming of the Shrew* published in 1623.

▼ Nevo, Ruth, 'Kate of Kate Hall' in *Modern Critical Interpretations of The Taming of the Shrew'*, Harold Bloom (ed.), New York: Chelsea House, 1988.

  — Nevo sees Katherine as a foil to Petruchio and that due to Petruchio's actions she is able to see herself, understand herself and change for the better due to her obvious intelligence. This reading does not view Katherine's will as having been broken but presents her as an (eventually) willing partner in change.

▼ Rebhorn, Wayne A. 'Petruchio's "Rope Tricks": *The Taming of the Shrew* and the Renaissance Discourse of Rhetoric', *Modern Philology* 92, No. 3, February 1995.

  — Rebhorn examines the play from the point of view of rhetoric, which, to Rebhorn, is the art of persuading someone to your way of thinking and sees the reference to 'rope-tricks' in *The Taming of the Shrew* as a 'textual crux'.

▼ Roberts, Jeanne Addison, 'Horses and Hermaphrodites: Metamorphoses in *The Taming of the Shrew'*, *The Shakespeare Quarterly* 34, No. 2, 1983.

  — Following a Classicist path, Roberts identifies *The Taming of the Shrew* with Ovid's *Metamorphoses* claiming that, in Shakespeare, metamorphoses improve characters. Roberts finds that Katherine's language in Act 4, scene 4 reflects Salmacis' speech to Hermaphroditus in Ovid: in the same way that Salmacis and Hermaphroditus merge into one being so do Katherine and Petruchio who mount their horses and ride to Padua together.

▼ Rutter, Carol, 'Kate, Bianca, Ruth, and Sarah: Playing the Woman's Part in *The Taming of the Shrew'* in *Shakespeare's Sweet Thunder: Essays on the Early Comedies*, Michael J. Collins (ed.), Newark: University of Delaware Press, 1997.

  — Rutter analyses the 'lording' of Sly in tandem with the 'taming' of Katherine and concludes that both transformations are wish-fulfilments not linked to any notions of human reality. Rutter makes use of the play's performance history to arrive at her conclusions.

▼ Thomas, Sidney, 'A Note on the *Taming of the Shrew'*, *Modern Language Notes*, Vol. 64, No. 2, February 1949.

  — Thomas compares *The Taming of a Shrew* with *The Taming of the Shrew* from an Elizabethan acting perspective and, among other things, finds some interesting things to say about Grumio.

▼ Wells Slights, Camille, 'The Raw and the Cooked in *The Taming of the Shrew*, *Journal of English and Germanic Philology* 88, 1989.

– The author, dissatisfied with readings that focus on the relationship between Katherine and Petruchio as obsessed with the idea of 'romantic love', claims the play has more to say about satire and the realities of Elizabethan social life.

▼ Wentersdorf, Karl, 'The Authenticity of *The Taming of the Shrew*', *Shakespeare Quarterly*, Vol. 5, No. 1, Jan., 1954.

(See also Wentersdorf's companion piece 'The Original Ending of *The Taming of the Shrew*: A Reconsideration', *Studies in English Literature* 18, 1978.)

– Wentersdorf argues that Shakespeare did write some concluding scenes to the play featuring Sly and that the play as it stands is an 'abridgement' of the playwright's original fair copy. This abridged version is the result of either an omission from the manuscript handed to the printer of the First Folio (such as the last page being missing) or is the consequence of the original editors Hemings and Condell believing Shakespeare had sanctioned the cuts during his lifetime.